The Apocalypse of Being

The Apocalypse of Being

The Esoteric Gnosis of Martin Heidegger

Mario Enrique Sacchi

Foreword by Ralph McInerny
Translation by Gabriel Xavier Martinez

ST. AUGUSTINE'S PRESS
South Bend, Indiana
2002

1 2 3 4 5 6 08 07 06 05 04 03 02

Library of Congress Cataloging in Publication Data
Sacchi, Mario Enrique, 1945–
    [Apocalipsis del ser. English]
    The apocalypse of being: the esoteric gnosis of Martin
    Heidegger / by Mario Enrique Sacchi; translated by Gabriel
    Martinez; foreword by Ralph McInerny.
        p.   cm.
    Includes bibliographical references and index.
    ISBN 1-890318-04-3 (alk. paper)
    1. Heidegger, Martin, 1889–1976. 2. Ontology – History –
    20th century. 3. Metaphysics – History – 20th century.
    I. Title.
    B3279.H49 S2713 2001
    193 – dc21   2001001190

Printed on acid free paper.

Printed in the Czech Republic by Newton Printing Ltd.   www.newtonprinting .com

For RALPH MCINERNY
eminent philosopher
and dear friend

TABLE OF CONTENTS

Foreword

The Apocalypse of Being provides English-language readers
with a good introduction to Mario Enrique Sacchi. Editor of
the prestigious Argentine review, *Sapientia*, which he has
turned into a truly international journal, Sacchi displays a
catholic interest in contemporary developments in philosophy and brings to their assessment a Catholic mentality,
steeped in the intellectual and cultural patrimony of the West.
Many who would identify themselves in the latter have
shown a remarkable receptivity to the thought of Martin
Heidegger. In this book, Sacchi scrutinizes the pillars of
Heideggerian thought and finds them unable to sustain the
edifice that has been elevated on them.

Heidegger's abiding and fundamental assumption is that
the whole history of western metaphysics is based upon a
mistake. Somewhere in the remote past of pre-Socratic philosophy, a wrong turn was taken and, to employ an
Aristotelian phrase, a small mistake in the beginning became
exponentially greater with time. What was lost was Being and
what became established was onto-theology. Recently, there
have been discussions of whether or not Thomas Aquinas
falls within the target area of Heidegger's critique.

Mario Enrique Sacchi's approach to Heidegger is radical.
He confronts the basic assumptions of the German philosopher's thought, and finds them to be increasingly obscure
assertions rather than proofs. More radically still, he charges

that Heidegger's "Thought about Being" is not philosophical discourse in any recognizable sense of the term. This makes it extremely difficult to make a philosophical appraisal of Heidegger's critique of metaphysics. The gnostic and vatic tone of the late Heidegger further undercuts the effort to take his sweeping claims seriously. Sacchi's book is, then, as severe a critique of Heidegger as one is likely to find, rivaling that of Stanley Rosen in his book *Nihilism*. But the intent of Sacchi's study is positive.

Metaphysics as represented by Saint Thomas Aquinas, unscathed by the Heideggerian critique, is presented as the great achievement of the philosophical quest. Traditional metaphysics has never had a better advocate than Mario Enrique Sacchi. I am delighted to present this book to readers of English and hope that it will be the first of many translations of his writings.

Ralph McInerny

Preface to the English Translation

The most significant problem in appraising accurately Martin Heidegger's thought lies in the meaning of what he called *Sein*. Certainly, this German noun is closely related to *being*, the metaphysical word par excellence. But what signification do metaphysicians attribute to the word *being*? It is well known that this question involves a very complicated semantic problem, a problem that comes to the fore in the English version of this book. Its translation from Spanish should enable us to overcome the great difficulty prevalent in all Latin languages, i.e., the ambivalent use of the noun *being*. However, the ambivalent use of *being* is not a pure and simple grammatical problem, for it also brings prejudice to the fortune of metaphysical speculation.

The complexity of the modern philosophical use of the word *being* is evident in its derivation from the two Greek and Latin verbs and of another two substantives of these classical languages. The Greek verb εἰμί signifies *to be*. The infinitive of this verb is ἐιναι, but some ancient Greek philosophers also used it as a noun to signify the act of being: τὸ ἐιναι. For instance, in a notable passage of his *Metaphysics*, Aristotle says that the principles of eternal things are causes of the act of being of non-eternal or worldly things.[1] This text synthesizes

---

1   Cf. Metaphys., Bk. II, ch. 1: 993 b 28–31.

masterfully two capital doctrines of Aristotle's metaphysics. On the one hand, he affirms here that the entity of all effects depends on their first principles and causes, which implies an unambiguous doctrine of creation *ex nihilo*, for the term 'creation' means nothing but the dependence of everything on a first principle of being. On the other hand, the same paragraph includes a tacit demonstration of God, one that St. Thomas Aquinas quoted as the philosophical argument on which his famous *quarta via* is based.[2]

Aristotle's theory has been misinterpreted by those who thought that the act of being would have no place in his first philosophy, as Étienne Gilson himself did. Gilson stood out among Neo-Thomist philosophers who argued emphatically for the absence, or at least on the scarce importance, of the notion of act of being in Aristotelian metaphysics. He pointed out that Aristotle "knew very well that being would be to be in act," and, as a consequence, "to be a being in act," but "to say what would be an act" would have been beyond the reach of Aristotle's philosophy.[3] Nevertheless, it is the case that, according to Aristotle, *to be* would not be restricted *to be in act* because, among many other divisions of being, he divided it into *being in act* and *being in potency*. It is obvious that in Aristotelian metaphysics, to be in potency is one of the modes of being. No doubt, Gilson's position is founded on his mistaken opinion about the non-existential nature of substance – the first category of predicamental being – as it is treated in the *Corpus aristotelicum*. In a recent article, Ralph McInerny showed a contradiction in Gilson's belief about the supposed non-existential character of Aristotelian substance.[4] The French thinker always insisted that in a realist philosophy there is no need for a demonstration of the existence of the

---

2   Cf. *Summ. theol.* I q. 2 a. 3c.

3   E. Gilson, *L'être et l'essence* (Paris: Librairie Philosophique Joseph Vrin, 1948), p. 50. Author's translation.

4   Cf. R. McInerny, "Do Aristotelian Substances Exist?" *Sapientia* 54 (1999) 325–38.

outside world.[5] Then, McInerny asks, why did he accuse
Aristotle of keeping silent about the existence of things whose
being in act is clearly evident to the human mind, as in the
case of material or sensible substances? In contradictory fashion, Gilson argued from Aristotle's metaphysics to the super-
fluity of verifying the existence of substances while criticizing
Descartes' idealistic gnoseology for failing to demonstrate
that substances have a positive mode of being outside man's
soul. By any reckoning, Gilson's explanation of the
Aristotelian conception of the act of being involves not only
an untenable misunderstanding of the Philosopher's own
theory, but also a veiled, although implicit, suspicion about
the fidelity of Aquinas' exegesis of Aristotle's contribution to
first philosophy. To admit Gilson's interpretation of
Aristotle's metaphysics requires that one also set aside St.
Thomas' own interpretation because of its now apparent
naïveté.

The right English translation of the Greek noun ἔιναι is
not *being* because the act of being of composed things does
not identify itself with the subject that exercises it. The subject
that is or exercises the act of being is signified by the neuter
participle ὄν, a thing that is or is being. That is why the substantive ὄν signifies *being*, a thing that is or is being, now in
act, now in potency. Something similar can be seen in Latin.
The Latin verb *sum* signifies *to be*, whose infinitive is *esse*, but
this infinitive is also used as a substantive to signify the act of
being, whereas the participle *ens* signifies that which exercises
the *esse* or the *actus essendi*. Hence the substantival form of *ens*
signifies *being* properly, i.e., the subject that is or is being.

Now, the English noun *being* cannot avoid the troubles
due to its ambivalent use in signifying indistinctly both the
subject (ὄν, *ens*) that exercises the act of being and the very act
of being (τὸ ἔιναι, *esse* or *actus essendi*) exercised by this subject. The problem is that no English word signifies explicitly
the act of being. As a result, the substantive *being* is ordinarily

---

5   Cf. E. Gilson, *Le réalisme méthodique* (Paris: Pierre Téqui, s.d.), *passim*.

used to signify, without any discrimination, both the subject that is and its own act of being.

A similar problem is found in Spanish, Italian, and French; not because these languages lack words to signify distinctly both being and the act of being, but because the infinitives *ser, essere,* and *être* have also been generally used as substantives to mean both that which is and the act by which it is. So, the term *the human being* is wrongly, although customarily, translated into Spanish as *el ser humano,* into Italian as *l'essere umano,* and into French as *l'être humain.* But this way of speaking is simply not justified. There are no reasonable motives in the aforesaid languages for leaving aside the grammatical diversity of nouns which signify *being* and *act of being.* Undoubtedly the ambivalent use of the substantives *ser, essere,* and *être* – which signify always the act of being (τὸ ἐιναι, *esse*) – leads to the easily avoidable confusion of this act with the subject that exercises it. The Spanish and Italian noun *ente,* and the French *étant,* in signifying invariably the subject that is or is being, allow their use duly distinguished from the meaning of those substantives which signify the act of being exercised by its subject. However, such a confusion does not happen in German language for here there is no problem of signifying the act of being by means of the substantiation of the infinitive of the verb *sein,* so that in German this act is called *Sein,* whereas its subject is not the *Sein* itself, but the *Seiende.* In this respect, one realizes that the strict observance of these grammatical rules by German philosophers proved rather useful when they were applied to metaphysical discourse.

In the light of these semantic criteria, metaphysicians who write in English have many difficulties in refering to the act of being. Which English word signifies appropriately what the ancient Greek philosophers called ἐιναι and those writing in Latin called *esse,* or *actus essendi*? There is no such English word. We can refer to the act of being by alluding to the ἐιναι of ὄν, to the *esse entis* or *actus essendi,* to *el ser del ente,* to *l'essere dell'ente*, to *l'être de l'étant*, and to *das Sein des Seienden*, but we cannot speak about *the being of being* for it is a term as metaphysically unintelligible as grammatically nonsensical.

The English language, however, offers two possibilities for surmounting this problem without falling into the equivocal and abstruse reiteration of a *being of being* and, yet plainly distinguishing the act from the subject that exercises such an act. Some contemporary philosophers have suggested the adoption of the term *the 'to be'* to signify both the Greek substantive εἰναι and the Latin one *esse* or *actus essendi*, but such a term is entirely foreign to the catalogue of usual English linguistic expressions. It is therefore afflicted with a patent unpopularity and with an exotic character. An alternative has become more acceptable, viz. the translation of εἰναι and *esse* as *act of being* and the preservation of the substantive *being* to signify only the subject that exercises this act. Although *act of being* is not a term of an everyday use, not even in philosophical milieus – except for Scholastic philosophy – no other terms are better able to signify the act of things that are or exercise such an act.

These clarifications are necessary for the truthful understanding of the title of this work. The title *The Apocalypse of Being* is not out of tune with the spirit of this book. Somebody might suggest that *The Apocalypse of the Act of Being* would be the best title. However, the former was chosen because this work deals with Heidegger's description of something he called "das Offenbarung des Seins," but this German term cannot be translated adequately as "the revelation of the act of being." The Heideggerian use of *Sein* is not compatible with the concept of act of being as it has been inherited from Aristotelian philosophical tradition and from mediaeval Scholastic philosophy. Heidegger thought that *Sein* is not a being, but, on the other hand, his *Sein* is not the act of being either. Not being the act of being, Heidegger's *Sein* is necessarily *aliquid*, something, or, against his own wishes, a certain being, for an *aliquid* is something convertible to a being or to a thing that is. In a word, Heidegger's *Sein*, at all events, would be a transcendental, but the act of being is not counted among those things called *transcendentalia* by mediaeval Scholastic metaphysicians. In fact, all that which is not the act of being is a being *entified* by this act. Let us explain now what meaning we confer on the verb *to entify*.

The Spanish verb *entificar* has been used as a neologism in the original text of this book to signify "to make that something be." For instance, the Thomistic metaphysical statement "God causes everything composed of essence and act of being," may also be enunciated by means of another which expresses the same theory: "God entifies everything whose essence is not its act of being." So, "to entify" signifies "to bestow the act of being," or "to produce a being as something that is." Once and for all, the proper function of the act of being is to give the first actuality to everything that is. In this way, we may affirm that *entification* is the formal effect of the act of being, that is to say to cause a being as such, or as a thing that is.

We hope readers do not consider the invention of the verb *to entify* and the substantive *entification* a disrespectful intrusion carried out by someone whose native language is not English. Our aim is only to offer a modest contribution in order to signify explicitly that which is called ἐιναι in Greek and *esse* or *actus essendi* in Latin. We are aware that, in doing so, someone might wonder why we did not use the noun *existence* as a synonym for *act of being*. Quite simply *to be* does not mean exactly *to exist*, neither in the complete range nor in the deepest intensity of their significations. The distinction between the act of being and the existence, or between *esse* and *existentia*, is a major problem of metaphysics. But the inquiry into the meaning of the concept of existence and of its relationship with the notion of act of being exceeds the scope of this work.

In the light of these statements, readers can understand why we needed to attend to the different significations of the three words most frequently mentioned in this book. In our text *being* means always the subject that is or exercises the act of being (τὸ ὄν, ens); *act of being* is the translation of *esse* and *actus essendi*, the act by means of which a thing is or is being (τὸ ἐιναι, *esse*) and the German noun *Sein*, such as Heidegger used it constantly, has been chosen to signify what he wished to designate with this same substantive, be that as it may.

Furthermore, we realize that some philosophers would object to our use of the term *act of being* for the nouns ἐιναι and *esse*, although it is the right translation of these Greek and Latin substantives. Of course, there is some inconvenience with this terminology. Firstly, the term *act of being* contains a certain ambiguity for it means both the *actus essendi* and the *actus entis*. And secondly, no one denies that the term *act of being* is not sufficiently common in philosophical milieus, to such an extent that it is almost exclusively restricted to metaphysical semantics of Scholasticism. Now, the first objection proceeds grammatically; namely, that it has no justifiable correlate *in rebus* because the act of being, without exception, is always the proper act of a determinate thing – being – that exercises it and by means of which every being is something that is, so that in the end both terms *actus essendi* and *actus entis* signify the very same act. The second objection is almost irrelevant because Scholastic philosophers are not to blame for the widespread neglect of metaphysical speculation on the act of being among their non-Scholastic colleagues. There are no compelling reasons for not using the terminology we have chosen. Metaphysicians do not use this term as a prosthesis nor as a camouflage to mask something mysterious and ineffable. In this sense, the metaphysical use of the term *act of being* is not a so-called "strategy" in order to display a philosophical diplomacy that is at odds with the strictness of first philosophy, the *domina scientiarum*. Contrary to the claims of Jean-Luc Marion, St. Thomas was a prominent champion of first philosophy and his constant reference to God's *esse* was not a "tactical" expedient to keep a cunning dialogue with

Scholastic, Arab, and Jewish philosophers and theologians in the Middle Ages.[6] After all, there is a capital difference between metaphysics and machination.

In this book we try to explain what is the revelation of *Sein* in Heidegger's writings. Of course, the apocalyptic disclosure of Heideggerian *Sein* has nothing to do with man's natural apprehension of the act of being nor with metaphysical knowledge of this same act. His opinion about the apocalyptic manifestation of *Sein* implies a complete rejection of metaphysics and its intended substitution by something he called *Denken*. But this "thinking of *Sein*," not being itself the metaphysical understanding of the act of being, rather consists of a cogitation which does not belong to the Western philosophical tradition that began with Plato and Aristotle. Thus, once the Heideggerian *Sein* would be something revealed enigmatically to human consciousness, it maintains a permanent sympathetic liaison with man's thought rather than with beings, since they hide it irremediably.

Not thinking about *Sein* as the act of being, Heidegger has been compelled to replace metaphysics by a strange thought unconcerned about natural beings, for their entities are supposedly entirely indifferent to this *Sein* which does not exhibit any causality with regard to themselves. Heidegger's *Sein* is neither the essence of the first uncaused cause nor the first active principle participated intrinsically in finite things entified by the act of being. That is why several metaphysicians have deemed that, in the end, his description of *Sein* is an esoteric gnosis fitted into a framework whose poles are a hermetic revelation, or an apocalyptic manifestation to human consciousness, and a nothingness which would determine inexorably the horizon of its wordly finitude. Although this estimation is severe, it is not mistaken.

I wish to express my warmest thanks both to Mr. Gabriel Martínez for translating this book into English and to

---

6   Cf. J.-L. Marion, "Saint Thomas d'Aquin et l'onto-théologie": *Revue Thomiste* 95 (1995) 64.

Dr. Timothy L. Smith, of Thomas Aquinas College, Santa Paula, California, for his kind review of this translation. I am aware of the difficulties both ought to face in putting the Spanish text of this work into a suitable form for English readers. I am also greatly indebted to Dr. Ralph McInerny, to whom this book is cordially dedicated, for the Foreword he so kindly wrote. I am also very grateful to Mr. Bruce Fingerhut, who was kind enough to publish the text through St. Augustine's Press.

Mario Enrique Sacchi
Buenos Aires, October 25, 2001

Prologue

Anyone attempting a philosophical evaluation of Martin Heidegger's thinking about *Sein* is liable to be disappointed. Heidegger is one of many modern authors who have systematically constructed a deliberately obscure thinking on *Sein*. Indeed, Heideggerian thought on *Sein* involves a particularly refined obscurity that cannot be understood without first learning its spiritual background. Yet such learning in the end is little more than an initiatory propaedeutic. It is not surprising then to find that in order to express his thinking on *Sein*, Heidegger had to invent an eccentric glossary. In so doing, he had to abandon almost completely the meaning of traditional philosophical terms and incorporate into his system others whose meaning he fixed *ad placitum* to make them conform to his peculiar thought on *Sein*.

This esotericism in Heideggerian thought on *Sein* raises the question of whether it belongs properly to philosophy or is of another kind, that is, non-philosophical. This doubt is not unjustified. If his thought on *Sein* wanted to be a proper philosophical thought, why would Heidegger revile Western metaphysics as a whole, the only science capable of dealing philosophically with the act of being? Once he was convinced that *Sein* could not be thought within the framework of the science of being as such, Heidegger tried to build a new thought on *Sein*. But the extra-metaphysical character of this

thought clearly implies its exile from philosophy, so that whoever thinks on *Sein* as Heidegger proposed it could not be
considered a philosopher. Of course, an extra-metaphysical
thought on *Sein*, whatever its character, is not a thought of a
formal philosophical nature.

It is commonly held that when Heidegger burst onto the
twentieth-century philosophical scene, he was considered the
thinker par excellence on the act of being, at least the so-called
"later Heidegger," who spoke of *Sein* incessantly and so
caused an unusual stir among members of the philosophical
guild. Nevertheless, in our opinion, an important aspect of
Heideggerian thought has not been seriously considered,
namely, that rather than being a thinker who dealt with the
act of being, Heidegger was a thinker who dealt with a
thought on *Sein*. Hence, his works reveal an undeniable interest in *Sein* interwoven with a concern for the *thinking* about
Sein.

From this point of view, it seems appropriate to note that
Heideggerian thought on *Sein* is in large measure an anachronistic restoration of Parmenides's primitive ontology. It has
been transposed in our age into the main concern of the
human spirit – already eloquently proclaimed by Hegel, the
champion of modern monist thought –, viz. to think and to be
are the same. In following Hegel's footsteps, Heidegger considers *Sein* and thinking in such a way that he is led to assert
that they are far more determinate than a simple correlation
might suggest. But Parmenides, in spite of having lived in the
inaugural stage of philosophizing – a time when the deep and
precise meaning of the act of understanding exercised by
intellect had not been fully grasped –, did not assert that the
act of being has its correlate in thought itself, but in the act
nominally signified by the verb voέω that is, in intellection: "It
is the same thing to understand and to be."[1] Ultimately,
Heideggerian thought on *Sein* is a thought on a thought about

---

1   H. Diels, *Die Fragmente der Vorsokratiker*, 28 B 3, 12th ed. by W. Kranz
(Dublin & Zürich: Weidmann, 1966), vol. I, p. 231. My translation.

a *Sein* thought by thought. But our author has left in the shadows the specification of this act that fascinates and captivates modern man, namely, thought itself. In spite of having written several works with the explicit intention of stipulating what this act is, neither in these nor in any others did Heidegger offer a satisfactory explanation of what thought is.[2]

Now, if Heideggerian thought on *Sein* is presented as something estranged from metaphysical speculation, why do we examine it from an explicitly metaphysical perspective? What profit would first philosophy derive from applying itself to an inquiry into a thinking foreign to its epistemic range? An honest answer to these questions requires one to ascertain the contradiction underlying Heidegger's thought on *Sein*, that is, although the core of such a thought on *Sein* is untenable from a metaphysical standpoint, not all of Heidegger's assertions on *Sein* are erroneous. Some truth, as little as it may be, hides in his tangled thoughts on *Sein*, for almost no effort of human reason, even if flawed by grave deviations, can result in the chaos of absolute falsehood. Therefore, we must thank him for the gift of his thought on *Sein*; not to accept the errors it hides, but to take advantage of his indefatigable endeavors for the sake of a true knowledge of the act of being. This is the best tribute we can offer to one who, paradoxically, plays the historic role of exceptional metaphysician *per accidens* in his frustrated attempt to substitute for first philosophy a thinking on *Sein* that, in spite of his opinions, can only occur within the theoretical framework of the science of being as such.

Heideggerian thought on *Sein* is not nourished by scientific theorizing about the things that are. On the contrary, it is

---

2   Cf. "Was heißt Denken?" in *Vorträge und Aufsätze*, 5th ed. (Pfullingen: Günther Neske, 1985), pp. 123–37; *Was heißt Denken?* 3rd ed. (Tübingen: Max Niemeyer, 1971); *Aus der Erfahrung des Denkens* (Tübingen: Max Niemeyer, 1954); "Grundsätze des Denkens," *Jahrbuch für Psychologie und Psychotherapie* 8 (1958) 33–41; *Zur Sache des Denkens* (Tübingen: Max Niemeyer, 1969); and *passim*.

an apocalyptic thought, since Heidegger has unequivocally stated that this thought depends on an epiphany of *Sein* that *reveals* it to thought itself. One of the most serious impediments to granting that such a thought is formally philosophical is found in this supposed revelation of *Sein*, since philosophy does not take its principles from any revelation, but from the natural evidence of intelligible things first known through sense experience that precedes every apprehension of our intellect. Moreover, the apocalyptic quality which, according to Heidegger, envelopes the manifestation of *Sein* to thought forces one to ask whether his thought on *Sein*, steadfastly set apart from the scientific tradition of Western philosophy, is not ultimately a gnosis of openly esoteric roots and of unpredictable spiritual outlook. On the other hand, Heideggerian gnosis has not introduced any substantial innovation into contemporary thought, which is itself long accustomed with such sources, since it ceased to be a speculation about things as such and gave in to the enchantment produced by the glitter of the knowing subject's self-consciousness.

We do not have at present a detailed analysis of the Gnostic character of modern man's thought. Many of its proposals are filled to bursting with a Gnosticism that penetrates them to their very marrow; on the other hand, only in the light of their chimerical triviality can we see the roots of such ravings. Ravings, certainly, because modernity's gnosis is not a mere list of fallacies, but a system dominated by the eagerness to give free rein to uncontrolled discourse and usually abetted by a dilettantism opposed to the serenity and rigor of the true philosophical spirit. Today there are not few who see in Heideggerian thought on *Sein* a typical intellectual model of modern Gnostic rambling.

We have little hope that these pages will satisfy either the sympathizers or the detractors of Heideggerian thought. They have been written with the conviction that metaphysics, defined and developed in an exemplary and still unsurpassed way by Aristotle and Saint Thomas Aquinas, is endowed with such indelible solidity that the Heideggerian attacks against the science of common being do not succeed in disrupting the coherence and the permanence of its teaching. This is not, therefore, a work aimed at setting forth integrally and exhaustively the Fribourg philosopher's thinking.[3] Its one aim is to expose the consequences of his rejection of the metaphysical understanding of being as such and of the act by which all the things that are exist. Among these consequences, to my mind, there is one that reveals the unfortunate consequence of Heidegger's attempt to replace first philosophy by an extra-metaphysical thought on *Sein*: the claudication of the human spirit, which is naturally ordered to acquiring the perfection of philosophical wisdom, out of a desire to liberate philosophical reason from the need to make use of a strict and inflexible syllogistic. The consequence of that claudication is made clear by the pretension to substitute for philosophy a radically non-scientific thought.

Governed by an intemperate affectivity, in Heidegger's hands the thought on *Sein* finally becomes an ornamental poetics in order to describe history aesthetically as the theater in which we find the drama of a man who despairs of knowing God by understanding created things in the world around us, i.e., *per ea quae facta sunt* (*Rom.* 1:20). Into Heidegger's world the rational animal has been strangely thrown having no possibility of transcending his presumed condemnation to suffer the tragedy of an implacable finitude destined to end in annihilation.

Not attempting, then, a historiographic inquiry into Heidegger's thought, we will try in this book only to expose its collision both with the science of being as such and with the metaphysical conclusions about the act of being of that which is. This is the one intended purpose of the text that the benevolent reader has now before his eyes. This is also the

---

3   The elucidations included in this book have been advanced in a shortened way in our article "La metafísica a pesar de Heidegger," *Sapientia* 54 (1999) 263–96.

reason why the quotations of the German philosopher's works have been reduced to a minimum, assuming that the reader already has sufficient knowledge of the whole of these writings to understand our criticism of Heidegger's thought on *Sein*. On the other hand, it is superfluous to say that this criticism has been carried out in the name of metaphysics itself. After all, Heidegger's rejection of metaphysics failed insofar as he did not accept the proper definition of the φιλοσοφία πρώτη, the science of being as such.

I dedicate with pleasure this book to Dr. Ralph McInerny, member of the Pontifical Roman Academy of Saint Thomas Aquinas, professor at the University of Notre Dame, and the true *chef d'école* of the Thomistic movement in the United States. May this be a modest homage to his vast and valuable work, which deservingly stands out in the present philosophical panorama, and to the cordial friendship with which he honors me.

Mario Enrique Sacchi
Buenos Aires, May 29, 1999

Chapter I

Martin Heidegger's Dispute with Metaphysics

The human spirit is profoundly and joyfully moved by contemplating the perfection reason attains in its tireless investigation of the truth of things. The perfection of reason does not lie merely in its discursive activity, or purely in the exercise of its proper act, but in the crowning of this act by the understanding of truth, for if reason does not reach an understanding of the truth of things, its discourse would not be perfected. Even more, since rational discourse can be frustrated by falling into error, discourse alone does not assure the acquisition of the truth sought because, as is well known, error results from disordered reasoning.

Nobody can sensibly deny that man's reason has attained innumerable and magnificent truths. Human science – which includes all knowledge obtained by means of apodictic argumentation exercised by the rational animal throughout history – is a trustworthy witness of man's eminence above all creatures existing in this world. But what is science but the truth contained in the soul, or the intentional correlate of the very truth of things apprehended demonstratively by our mind? Scientific knowledge possessed by man's possible intellect – not in vain called "the place of species" (τόπος εἰδών) by the ancient Greek philosophers[1] – is the truth attained thanks to the immaterial union of the intellect with the objects known through the exercise of its apprehensive acts. Moreover, since knowledge cannot be false, science as such is essentially true because a false knowledge is absolutely impossible.

Nevertheless, it is not only the nobility of the truth that moves the human spirit. It is also moved, not with joy, but with sadness, by realizing that true knowledge is sometimes disdained in favor of a sort of prevarication committed by reason in using its natural perceptive capacity. Note the seriousness of this attitude: science is always a true knowledge attained by human reason's inferences duly rectified by the liberal art of logic. Sometimes, however, reason is treated with contempt because in spite of having attained scientific knowledge, it is accused of having acted improperly in inspecting its objects with the assistance of logic. Above all, the seriousness of this attitude can be seen in the denial that the science achieved by human reason has the character of a true knowledge, i.e., when it is denied that science itself is truly a science. But the seriousness of this attitude reaches an extreme degree when the denial of the status of true science not only affects any epistemic understanding immanent to the human intellect, but also the supreme science acquired by our intellect through the virtuous exercise of its natural forces, viz. metaphysics or first philosophy, the old and roughly handled science of being as such, which the wisest men always considered the *domina scientiarum*.

History reports numerous attacks against metaphysics. The Modern Age itself has been the scenario of one onrush after another against first philosophy to such an extent that this age has become something of a battlefield on which our science has suffered an incessant siege from the legion of enemies who strove to eliminate it completely from the human soul. One of the last attempts still eagerly pursued by various

---

1   Cf. Aristotle, *De anima*, Bk I, ch. 4: 429 a 27-28.

rivals of first philosophy, may be summarized as follows: metaphysics is the science of being as such, but in dealing with this subject metaphysicians forgot to think on the act of being, which would remain lost in oblivion because it is hidden inside the being. First philosophy is purportedly impotent to deal with it insofar as this science concerns that being in which such act is concealed. Hence, we are told, the required thinking about the act of being is beyond the reach of the science of being as such.

In this statement one notices the contradiction implied in asserting that the subject of metaphysics is being as such and, at the same time, in denying that this science is a knowledge of the act of being presumably hidden and therefore imperceptible inside the being. This contradiction arises at the very instant a proper knowledge of its subject, being as such, is attributed to our science. This science is denied its epistemic fitness to know the act of being because supposedly the act is hidden inside the being, and man is thereby prevented from thinking about such an act. Where is the contradiction in this statement? Simply, in the impossibility of understanding being without understanding the act by which it is such a being, because being is something that is thanks to the act that determines it as a being. Furthermore, this act gives to every being its own reason of being insofar as such an act entifies everything that is, or in making it to be. Whoever knows a being, also knows that it is, and it is by the act of being. In fact, whoever does not know a being entified by the act of being, i.e., a being not entified, knows nothing. Something that is not, or a non-being, simply cannot be known, since it is a mere nothingness or something unknowable. To know something that is not, a nothingness, would imply not knowing anything.

The statement synthesized in the penultimate paragraph is intrinsically contradictory because metaphysics, the science of being as such, is the science of that which is insofar as it is. The terms of this statement involve the contradiction of assigning to metaphysics a knowledge of a given subject –

being in common – which cannot be known without an explicit understanding of the act of being because this act makes everything to be. In consequence, if someone affirms that metaphysics is the science of being as such but thinks that it does not attain to a knowledge of the act of being, he must deny immediately that there is a science of something understood as being that begins with the understanding of the act of being by which a being is a being.

The aforementioned statement also includes two additional contradictions. One of them lies in believing that metaphysics would not be a knowledge of the act of being which is hidden in being. Indeed, it is contradictory to assert that metaphysics is the science of being as such, or of that which is, and to assert at the same time that it could not know the cause by which a being is. But if metaphysics is a science of natural reason, and science is the certain knowledge of things through their causes,[2] then first philosophy can only be the science of being as such insofar as it involves the knowledge of the act of being by which everything that is is. Hence, in the final analysis, the rejection of metaphysical knowledge of the act of being also entails the rejection of metaphysics as the science of being as such. Even more, this position implicitly bolsters the position according to which metaphysics is neither a science nor a knowledge, because the intellect, as it was said above, cannot know a being without knowing the act that entifies it, or the act which makes it to be something that is and that is precisely what it is: a being. The second contradiction derives from the assertion of a supposed concealment of the act of being in being. Such concealment would prevent its perception through metaphysical intellection because being would hide the act of being, and this act would only be knowable independently from the intelligibility of the things that are, things that have an act of being. But it is clear that there is nothing intelligible beyond that which is, or beyond

---

2   Cf. Aristotle, *Analyt. post.* Bk. II, ch. 2: 71 b 9–12.

being itself, and so the act of being would only be knowable in an illusory kingdom of nothingness, where there is nothing, and therefore neither being. In short, if the act of being would be hidden in being, which is the subject of metaphysics, we could know neither the being that is by the act of being, nor the act by which everything is. But the impossibility of knowing that which is thanks to the act of being, and even the supposed concealment of this act in being would entail the unavoidable and absolute impossibility of knowledge itself. Everything that we can know is a being by virtue of the act of being that makes it something that is. There is nothing to know beyond that which is. That is why both the denial of metaphysics and the denial of metaphysical knowledge of the act of being imply an old and obstinate skeptical attitude. One inevitably falls into this attitude with these kinds of contradictions.

This criticism of metaphysics involves a vilification of the science of being as such that inheres in the human soul because philosophizing reason is applied to the knowledge of everything entified by the act of being. But are there reasons to impugn metaphysics by invoking a philosophical worry concerning its potency to know the act of being? It is well known that the following assumption underlies this criticism: human reason could establish that metaphysics has been unsuccessful in its attempts to think on the act of being because another thought, of a kind differing from first philosophy would be able to deal with this act and also with the very misstatements with which the science of being as such is reproached due to its frustrated endeavor to know that act. Then, such an extra-metaphysical thought would enable one to think on the act of being and to judge the epistemic solidity of our science which leaves the act of being in oblivion. Consequently, this extra-metaphysical thought on the act of being prides itself on being a thought superior beyond compare in relation to first philosophy.

Now, what is this extra-metaphysical thought that claims for itself the power to think on the act of being independently of the analytics of the science of being as such and even possess a scientific competency that would subject first philosophy to its own unappealable authority? In other words, is it a thought of a formal philosophical nature or, on the contrary, a thought whose apparent superiority in relation to metaphysics would require that it verges on a loftiness exceeding the scientific level of philosophy? If the latter, is it a thought similar to philosophical science attainable by man's reason in exercising his own natural powers, or failing that, a thought bound up with other kinds of human apprehensions of things, in the manner of artists' aesthetic ideation? or of mystics' contemplative-amatory experience? or of religious fables contrived by an imagery intended for sublimating mythical deities invented by human fantasy?

The proposed view is reduced to a dialectics that put aside every speculation on the act of being in the framework of the science of being as such and defends the necessity of grasping it through a thought which does not belong to the field of philosophy or to the apodictic working of natural reason. Again, proposing this extra-metaphysical thought on the act of being entails a rejection of metaphysics provided that, in this case, the science of being as such would not inhere in our soul, as it has been argued, since the intellect does not know that act by understanding its common formal object – being itself. In that case, one must condemn all philosophy as a fiasco, a disappointment, or at least a deceit, because its consummation in metaphysical speculation on being as such ultimately fails. The ambition of thinking on the act of being as a pure act of being is finally frustrated by the inaccessibility of the act of being itself, concealed in the impenetrable darkness of being.

Then, what is this thought on the act of being that shows itself as a thought on the act of being in defiance of metaphysics and, moreover, segregated from a philosophical knowledge which is blamed for the worst crime that human reason may commit, that is, forgetting to think on the act of being which entifies everything that is? A frightening impression arises from the mere formulation of this question: we are faced with a thought that claims to be in possession of an exhaustive register of all the propositions about the act of being stated by human intellect throughout history, none of which, once examined by the supra-metaphysical authority of such a thought, would satisfy the requirements of an authentic thought about that entifying act. On the contrary, this thought would have appeared *post metaphysicam*, or just after the science of being as such was condemned to expiate the sin of the neglecting the act of being. But it contains something even more frightening, for this extra-metaphysical thought on the act of being does not draw inspiration from the truth of things that are – the truth of everything from which the concept of being is predicated, or from the truth of the very subject of first philosophy – but from a different source. From what source? If we were not able to think on the act of being through metaphysical understanding of being as such, because it would remain hidden to philosophizing reason, and if its philosophical oblivion would not allow us to think in it, this peculiar thought on the act of being substituting for the science of common being could not find inspiration in the truth of the things that are, things so fruitlessly studied by philosophy, particularly metaphysics. Necessarily, this thought on the act of being would originate in a revelation, in the revelation of the act of being itself to thought. Therefore, it would be a thought that, having proceeded from a revelation – that which in Greek language is called ἀποκάλυψις – would deserve to be understood as a correlatively apocalyptic thought.

Nevertheless, having noticed the source from which this extra-metaphysical thought on the act of being would come, our fear only increases as we become aware of another amazing datum that shows it in possession of a surprising claim that no metaphysician has granted to his own science: the ἀποκάλυψις, or the revelation of the act of being. Hitherto unknown to humanity and to the entire guild of philosophers through twenty-seven centuries of epistemic speculation, this revelation would be given to the one person who diagnosed both its concealment in the things that are and its negligence in metaphysics. Thus, the truth of the act of being in revealing itself to this one person would be disclosed, and this person would have the honor of rescuing it from oblivion.

All who are adequately acquainted with contemporary philosophy will readily see that these statements contain the core of Martin Heidegger's teachings developed in the later stage of his academic and literary career, which altogether spanned more than a half a century.

The dazzling aspect of Heidegger's thought, but also the most confused and devious and perhaps personifying the height of naïveté, lies in having claimed to be the repository of the revelation of something that he called *Sein*, which, in spite of its identity with the *esse* or *actus essendi*, is not the act of being of the metaphysical tradition. But the understanding of Heideggerian thought requires the elimination, or at least the moderation, of the somewhat arbitrary break between the "early Heidegger" and the "later Heidegger," or between the two stages of the development of his thought on *Sein*, which would bifurcate around the Second World War. The "Later Heidegger's" thought would have arisen from a turn (*Kehre*) in relation to the works of the "early Heidegger," who had granted previously an explicit privilege to the ontic preeminence of *Dasein*, or the human existent. In the later period, he devoted himself both to an enthusiastic exaltation of *Sein* and to the extra-metaphysical thought ordered to think about it. Nevertheless, regarding his points of view on *Sein*, it is more convenient to divide the development of Heidegger's thought into two other stages that do not coincide with those just noted above. First, however, we will reconsider the commonly accepted distinction between the "early" and "later Heidegger."

The first stage of Heidegger's thought started in 1912. Bonded to the German Catholic milieux that advocated the principles of Neoscholastic philosophy, he published his article "Das Realitätsproblem in der modernen Philosophie" in the journal *Philosophisches Jahrbuch* edited by the Görres Society of Fulda.[3] This article preceded some book reviews sent by Heidegger to the *Literarische Rundschau für das katholische Deutschland*.[4] In this stage he also wrote his dissertation on the theory of judgment in psychologism, prepared under the direction of Arthur Schneider. Because of this work he was granted the degree of doctor of philosophy from the University of Fribourg of Brisgovia.[5] Two years later he submitted to this same university his monograph on John Duns Scotus's doctrines of categories and signification, an essay concerning a mediaeval philosophical text up till then mistakenly attributed to the *Doctor Subtilis*. He was then awarded the post of *Privatdozent* of the same house of studies.[6] The

---

3   Cf. "Das Realitätsproblem in der modernen Philosophie": *Philosophisches Jahrbuch* 25 (1912) 353-363, reprinted in *Frühe Schriften*, ed. by F.-W. von Herrmann, in *Martin Heidegger: Gesamtausgabe* (Frankfurt am Main: Vittorio Klostermann, 1978 ff.), vol. I, pp. 1–15.

4   Cf. "Neu Forschungen über Logik": *Literarische Rundschau für das katholische Deutschland* 38 (1912): 466–72, 527–34 and 565–70; and the book reviews of N. von Bubnoff, *Kants Briefe: Zeitlichkeit und Zeitlosigkeit*; F. Brentano, *Von der Klassification physischer Phänomene*; Ch. Sentroul, *Kant und Aristoteles*; and F. Groß, *Kant-Laienbrevier*. See also *Frühe Schriften*, pp. 17–54.

5   Cf. *Die Lehre vom Urteil in Psychologismus: Ein kritisch-positiver Beitrag zur Logik* (Leipzig: Johann Ambrosius Barth, 1914), reprinted in *Frühe Schriften*, pp. 59-188.

6   Cf. *Die Kategorien- und Bedeutungslehre des Duns Scotus* (Tübingen: Verlag J. C. B. Mohr [Paul Siebeck], 1916), reprinted in *Frühe Schriften*,

publication of this monograph marked the end of the first stage of Heidegger's thought, who with these writings made his initial forays into philosophy as one of the many exponents – so he was considered at that time – of the Neoscholastic movement that stood out in Catholic European academia, especially after the closing of the First Ecumenical Vatican Council.

Heidegger had been introduced into Neoscholastic philosophy through his youthful approach to the Society of Jesus, which had a strong presence in academic circles at Fribourg. The University of Fribourg of Brisgovia had become a bastion of New Scholasticism in Germany thanks to the activity of erudite professors who pioneered and consolidated it during the second half of the nineteenth century and extended it firmly in the following. Among others, theologians and philosophers of the stature of Johann Baptist Hirscher, Franz-Anton Staudenmaier, Johann Baptist Alzog, Karl Braig, Joseph von Schätzler S.J., Joseph Geyser, etc. have shone in Fribourger classrooms.

Our insistence on the philo-Neoscholastic character of this first stage of Heidegger's thought is supported on many indisputable documents brought out by several scholars. A renowned treatise of philosophical historiography from the first decades of the twentieth century cites him as a German representative of the Neoscholasticism, a Catholic movement begun with the publication of Pope Leo XIII's encyclical *Aeterni Patris*, dated the 4 of August, 1879. It is also astonishing to see Heidegger named immediately after Martin

pp. 189–411. This dissertation follows the lines of the *Grammatica speculativa*, a work that in 1922 Msgr. Martin Grabmann restored to the authorship of Thomas of Erfurt with other medievalists' general approval. See M. Grabmann, "De Thoma Erfordiensi auctore Grammaticae quae Ioanni Duns Scoto adscribitur speculativae": *Archivum Franciscanum Historicum* 15 (1922) 273–77; and "Die Entwicklung des mittelalterlichen Sprachlogik (*Tractatus de modis significandi*)": *Philosophisches Jahrbuch* 35 (1922) 121–35 and 199–214.

Grabmann in one of the most highly esteemed contemporary treatises of the history of philosophy – the handbook written originally by Friedrich Überweg – in a section titled "Die Philosophie der katholischen Kirche: Der Neuthomismus."[7] Just a few years later, this estimation of the philosophical filiation of Heideggerian thought would be considered untenable.

The second stage of Heidegger's thought started to crystallize with the inclusion of *Sein und Zeit* in the philosophical yearbook edited by Edmund Husserl.[8] But between this stage and the former one Heidegger remained in a strange literary silence. What happened in those eleven years in which he published no work? In principle, this question has no philosophical motivation, for it is not unusual that a philosopher stops writing for a time only to write again later. But in Heidegger's case there is something that compels one to inquire about the causes of his literary silence from 1916 to 1927. *Sein und Zeit* makes clear that the philosopher previously bound to Catholic Neoscholasticism had been left behind definitively. Heidegger never explained the reasons that encouraged the development of his thought all along those eleven years. However, one can observe that in his turn from Neoscholasticism to phenomenological ontology, his thought incorporated some puzzling new elements, e.g., the *Seinsfrage* being dependent on the anthropological key inherent in his conception of the human being; the enunciation of the

---

7   "The relationships between Scholasticism and modern German logic and metaphysics have been expounded recently in an interesting way by M. *Grabmann* [...and by] M. *Heidegger*" (F. Überweg, *Grundriß der Geschichte der Philosophie*, vol. IV: "Die deutsche Philosophie des XIX. Jahrhunderts und der Gegenwart," 12th ed. by T. K. Österreich [Berlin: E. S. Mittler & Sohn, 1923], p. 642. My translation).

8   Cf. "Sein und Zeit: Erste Hälfte": *Jahrbuch für Phänomenologie und phänomenologische Forshung* 8 (1927) 1–446. Although this text was presented as the first part of a major work, Heidegger did no continuation of it, so that *Sein und Zeit*, at long last, remained such as it was edited by Husserl.

problem of *Sein* according to the questioning of the capacity of our intellect to know the things of the external world; the interference of affective factors such as anguish with philosophical understanding; the dependence of *Sein* on the one who asks for it, the cure (*Sorge*); the criticism of theoretical positions based on the message of Holy Scripture; the correlation of *Sein* and the activity of consciousness; the decision to indict entirely the history of metaphysics; etc. Nevertheless, it is not difficult to notice that these and other elements, which appeared unexpectedly in the philosophical stage of Heidegger's thought that started with *Sein und Zeit*, were already rooted in the peculiar absorption of agnostic occasionalism from Protestantism, which is permeated beyond all doubt with nominalism. Agnostic occasionalism was inserted in Protestantism since its very foundation in Luther's works, but reinforced later through the restatement of Reformed theology by Schleiermacher in the first half of the nineteenth century.

Consequently, if it is fitting to speak of an "early Heidegger" and of a "later Heidegger," it seems that the bifurcation of his thought on *Sein* did happen during his literary silence between 1916 and 1927, i.e., in the transitional period when his youthful thought, closer to Neoscholasticism, eventually accepted the parameters latent in the foundation of the Protestant spirit. The Protestant spirit, however, found expression in two rather different forms. On the one hand, a trend that started with Melanchthon shared to a great extent some features with the Scholastic tradition; so, parallel with the Catholic Scholastic movement, a Protestant Scholas-ticism had developed. Goclenius, Casmann, Clauberg, Leibniz, Wolff, and Baumgarten were its most outstanding exponents. On the other hand, another trend imbued with an openly affectivist emphasis, nearer to Luther's religious concerns, yielded in the construction of the theosophical mysticism spread by Heinrich Cornelius

Agrippa von Nettesheim, Johannes Scheffler – known much better through the pseudonymous of Angelus Silesius–, Sebastian Frank, Valentin Weigel, Jacob Böhme, Georg Gichtel, and Friedrich Ötinger.[9] Both trends came together in Kant's agnostic conceptualism and religious pietism. But Kant's work also contains the paradigm synthesis of transcendental philosophy, which Protestant culture betokened from its very beginning in the sixteenth century. Thenceforth Protestantism fitted together rationalist and affectivist sources that sustained it historically. But if the Kantian system, although with a delay of more than two centuries, acted as the philosophical foundation of Reformed Christianity, the consolidation of the Protestant theological program arose from an alliance of such a system with a mysticism that, in the nations where the Reform thrived, penetrated popular religiousness and reached mythological levels in the literature of some poet-theologians who were extolled as "fathers of the German soul." Klopstock, Goethe, Schiller, and Hölderlin stood out among these authors. Therefore, it is impossible to understand rightly the meaning of the subsequent development of Protestant thought if one does not take into account the conjunction of Kant's critical system with the mystification of Christianity cast into German folk mythology. Protestant thought thereby turned out to be the bulwark of a secularizing demolition of metaphysics from the end of the eighteenth century onward. Indeed, who would dare deny that both Kant's critical system and the mysticism of the aforementioned poet-theologians have been the cornerstones of Protestant fundamentalism professed by the theological, philosophical, political, and aesthetic luminaries in Germany since then, namely Fichte, Goethe, Hölderlin, Schiller,

---

9   Cf. F. Überweg, *Grundriß der Geschichte der Philosophie*, vol. III: "Die Philosophie der Neuzeit bis zum Ende des XVIII. Jahrhunderts," 12th ed. by M. Frischeisen-Köhler und W. Moog (Berlin: E. S. Mittler & Sohn, 1924), pp. 134–53.

Schelling, Schleiermacher, Hegel, Schopenhauer, Bismarck, Wagner, Nietzsche. . . ?

Heidegger obtained his first philosophical education in close contact with a Neoscholasticism in which the doctrine of Francisco Suárez dominated. The ponderous influence of Leibniz and Wolff did not overshadow Suárez, especially as they themselves held the *Disputationes metaphysicae* of the master from Granada in high esteem. By means of his Neoscholastic education Heidegger maintained a suggestive liaison both with Catholic and Protestant Scholasticism. But, as it was said above, a different Heidegger appeared when *Sein und Zeit* was published in 1927. This new Heidegger showed that his thought, after the literary silence of eleven years, adopted a direction that coincided clearly with those trends prevailing in the spirit of Protestantism as expressed in the German cultural milieux. In fact, in *Sein und Zeit* Heidegger expressed his aim to carry out an essential reform of philosophical tradition which goes back to Plato and Aristotle. With this aim he had recourse to Protestant transcendentalism, as it appeared in an exemplary fashion in the works of Kant and Hegel – both of them the preeminent Protestant philosophers – as well as in the peculiar artistic trappings of Hölderlin's neopagan mysticism. This poet captivated Heidegger, already moving away from New Scholasticism, in the same way as in the previous century he had charmed his friends Schiller, and Schelling, and also the most notable among all his friends: Hegel himself.[10]

Thus, Heideggerian thought on *Sein* has its roots in the Protestant ferment that since Luther's time has never ceased to proclaim the need to put a stop to the development of metaphysics, the science inserted in the heart of Western philosophy through the works of Plato and Aristotle. This science

---

10 Some interpreters of Hegelian thought are inclined to consider Hölderlin's influence on Hegel unimportant; e.g., W. Kaufmann, *Hegel* (Garden City, N.Y.: Doubleday, 1965), p. 36.

reached its height in mediaeval Scholasticism through the speculative exploits of St. Thomas Aquinas, which, according to the hermeneutic distortion of Thomism in Luther's works, had undermined the essence of Christianity by infiltrating it with Pelagian arrogance. However, since some currents of Protestant Scholasticism had preserved the metaphysical tradition in a sense that was not entirely out of keeping with the Catholic exegesis of first philosophy, the overcoming of this branch of knowledge that fails to think on *Sein* would require a refoundation of the thought ordered to think about it. So, having rejected the fitness of metaphysics to think on *Sein* as such, Heidegger echoed the Protestant agnostic fervor by demonstrating an open repudiation of philosophy itself. Indeed, a philosophy powerless to theorize on the act of being according to the analytics of the science of being as such would conceal a plain defrauding of the metaphysical vocation fixed in the rational animal's soul. In the face of this position, we must ask again: insofar as it is not a metaphysical thought, is Heideggerian thought on *Sein* a thought of a philosophical nature? Or, rather, to what extent does an extra-metaphysical thought on *Sein* belong to the heritage of philosophy?

Among philosophers, opinions are frequently subjected to extensive criticisms, sometimes biting and vehement. Heidegger's statements have not been spared from this rule. Nevertheless, it is remarkable that some philosophers not only have criticized his opinions, but have even cast doubt on their philosophical nature and, as a consequence, have cast doubt on the philosophical quality of the man who propounded them. Certainly, if this approach to Heideggerian thought sounds severe, his admirers, excited by the discrediting of Heidegger as an authentic philosopher, will manifest angrily their indignation. However, it was Heidegger himself who gave his critics reason to resist considering him an authentic philosopher. Doubtless, Heidegger himself scorned the capacity of philosophizing reason to know *Sein* through the apodictics of metaphysics, the sapiential crowning of philosophy. He also scorned the possibility of understanding *Sein* by inspecting things that are and attempted instead to experience it by means of a historical revelation. Furthermore, against the speculative tradition founded on the doctrines of the outstanding philosophers throughout history, Heidegger opposed the enthralling inspiration of some poets selected *ad libitum* from the German vernacular patrimony, beyond which no other exponents of human culture seemed to have interested him.

If Heidegger had wanted to structure a thought on *Sein* that prided itself on being of a veritable philosophical nature, he must have known for certain that there is no philosophy outside philosophy itself. A physician cannot be a physician if he neither knows nor practices medicine, nor can a musician be a musician if he neither knows nor practices music. In the same way, it is not possible to be a philosopher by attacking philosophy resentfully. Even less may someone be himself a philosopher if, once in possession of some of the greatest achievements of the philosophical sciences, he despises them in the name of a thought about *Sein* that purports to be philosophical and anti-philosophical at the same time. The inflexibility of the principle of non-contradiction, the supreme principle of intellectual life, does not tolerate transgressions of this kind. Thus, if there is no philosophy outside philosophy itself, even less can there be an anti-philosophical philosophy. Heideggerian thought on *Sein* may be considered to be philosophical on condition that the word *philosophy* be taken in an equivocal sense.

The rejection of the philosophical character of Heideggerian thought on *Sein* was insinuated almost immediately after the publication of *Sein und Zeit*. Neopositivism, also known as "Logical Positivism" or "Analytic Philosophy," which came into being with the Vienna Circle in the early

1920s, defied it expressly. Some authors in this movement criticized Heidegger's thought both for its separation from logic and for its persistence in the metaphysical tradition, which they believed to have had its highest exposition in Hegel. Of course, there is no basis for the latter appraisal since Heidegger, as it was said, has been one of the decisive opponents to the Western metaphysical tradition, in which Hegel's thought could only be considered an accidental representative. It is true that Heideggerian thought, under the influence of Protestant theology, had always shown strained relations with logic, at least since the publication of *Sein und Zeit*. In his article "Überwindung der Metaphysik durch logische Analyse der Sprache" of 1932, Rudolf Carnap accused Heidegger of having broken the fundamental laws of rational philosophy by dissolving his thought into meaningless propositions.[11] At the sight of the text of a lecture delivered by Heidegger on 24 July 1929 at the University of Fribourg of Brisgovia, Carnap accused him of distorting the usual signification of philosophical terms and, accordingly, in breaching the elementary propositions of logic. For instance, Heidegger used the noun *nothingness* as something which could be revealed by angst, but in Carnap's opinion this seems to refer to a certain thing bound to an emotion probably experienced under the weight of some worry of a religious character.[12] About the same time, Otto Neurath held the same opinion in

---

11   The German original of Carnap's article appeared in volume 2 (1931–1932) of *Erkenntnis*, a philosophical journal published in Leipzig from 1930 to 1938. Cf. R. Carnap, "The Elimination of Metaphysics through Logical Analysis of Language," translated by A. Pap, in A. J. Ayer (Ed.), *Logical Positivism* (Glencoe, Ill.: The Free Press, 1959), pp. 60–81.

12   Cf. R. Carnap, "The Elimination of Metaphysics through Logical Analysis of Language," *ibid.*, p. 71. It is obvious that Carnap alludes here to Heidegger's famous sentence that reads as follows: "The anguish reveals nothingness" (*Was ist Metaphysik?* 10th ed. [Frankfurt am Main: Vittorio Klostermann, 1969], p. 33, reprinted in *Wegmarken*,

his article "Protokollsätze."[13] Later Alfred Jules Ayer, the last
great representative of logical positivism, argued that
Heidegger, just as Berkeley and McTaggart in a previous age,
had expounded his ontological thought through several illogical devices which were little more than "pieces of ver-
biage."[14] Even more emphatically, in trying to refute the illogical of intuitionist thought, Mario Bunge noted that he saw in
Heideggerian intuitionism a "pathological symptom of mental rigidity and conceitedness" not unlike that of Husserl and
Scheler.[15]

The problem of the philosophical character of
Heidegger's thought, partially noted by Neopositivists, was
also pointed out by authors of different theoretical trends,
such as Ernst Cassirer, who in his posthumous book *The Myth
of the State* noted the illogical nature of Heidegger's doctrine.
According to Cassirer, Heidegger, though a disciple of
Husserl, did not persevere in the orientation that his master
imposed on phenomenological philosophy. Phenomenology
arose from a meticulous analysis of the principles of logical
thought, and its ulterior development depended entirely on
this analysis. Heideggerian thought is instead completely
adverse to the logical foundations of phenomenology; so
much so that for Heidegger, according to Cassirer's harsh
opinion, it would be useless "to try to build up a logical

2nd ed. [Frankfurt am Main: Vittorio Klostermann, 1978], p. 112. My
translation).

13   Cf. O. Neurath, "Protocol Sentences," translated by G. Schick, in A. J.
Ayer (Ed.), *Logical Positivism*, pp. 199–208. See especially p. 200.

14   A. J. Ayer, "Editor's Introduction" to *Logical Positivism*, p. 16. Cf. Id.,
Language, Truth and Logic, reprint (Harmondsworth: Penguin Books,
1971), p. 59.

15   "When it is not a sign of candor – as it was in the case of the moderate
intuitionism of traditional rationalists – philosophical intuitionism can
be a pathological form of mental rigidity and conceitedness, as illus-
trated by Husserl, Scheler, and Heidegger." (M. Bunge, *Intuition and
Science* [Englewood Cliffs: Prentice-Hall, 1962], p. 118).

philosophy."[16] But, if this is so, are there any reasons to consider a philosopher someone who is devoted to constructing
a thought intentionally permeated with the illogical?

Once Heidegger argued for the extra-metaphysical character of a thought on *Sein*, he was not able to avoid his self-
estrangement from philosophy. Nobody expelled him from
the philosophical guild, but he himself made the decision to
attempt a thought about *Sein* emancipated from the rules of
logic, unconcerned with the things of this world investigated
by natural sciences, and incompatible with the understanding
of being as such because he supposed that metaphysics
would absorb accumulatively the failure of Western philosophy in its fruitless thought on *Sein* as a pure *Sein*. Thus,
Heidegger's choice of a non-philosophical thought leads one
to ask what is this extra-metaphysical thought on *Sein* that
refuses to identify itself with a philosophical knowledge duly
rectified by the liberal art of logic and, as if that were not
enough, that also pretends to dispute the suitability of the science of common being to grasp it through an explicit speculation on this subject.

Heidegger bequeathed to posterity a thought about *Sein*
essentially different from scientific knowledge of a human
reason ordered to the understanding of the act by which is
everything that is, i.e., metaphysics. Heideggerian thought on
Sein is not the philosophical knowledge of the act of every act
and of the perfection of every perfection obtainable by our
apodictic reason. On the contrary, it is a meditation on something that could not be understood in the objectivity of a
being that would hide it. Inversely, it would be thinkable
insofar as it is received into consciousness by means of a revelation that would make it evident in the subjective intimacy
of thought itself. Nevertheless, in Heidegger's writings the
relations that the revelation of *Sein* would keep with thought
invariably show themselves dark and enigmatic, for he was

16   E. Cassirer, *The Myth of the State* (Garden City: Doubleday, 1965), p. 368.

always hesitant to settle whether it is a cognoscitive correlation, an affective conjunction, a productive and unitive otherness of terms bound among themselves in the fashion of a poetic dialogue, or a substantial identity of the thought on *Sein* with a *Sein* thought by thought itself, in which thought would think about itself by thinking the *Sein* revealed to consciousness as perhaps no more than to be thought.

Heidegger considered *Sein* to be something not apprehensible in things that are or in the intelligibility of being as such studied by metaphysicians. On one hand, it would require a revelation that would overlook absolutely the being in which *Sein* can only be concealed and forgotten by metaphysicians. On the other hand, *Sein* would also be the product of the task of a thought that would think on itself by focusing on its entire beinglessness.

However, the science acquired by philosophizing reason through the investigation of things that are by the act of being that makes them to be – an investigation that reaches its uppermost perfection in metaphysical knowledge – is not a knowledge which would depend on any revelation, but on an ἀπόδειξις ruled by the first indemonstrable principles of understanding. On the contrary, Heidegger wished to think about *Sein* subject to an ἀποκάλυψις, but he did not bring forward any evidence for this revelation. Moreover, he also did not prove that this revelation could be the starting point of the philosophical theorizing of man's epistemic reason, for philosophical speculation cannot be based on any revelation.

Let us ask once more: is Heidegger's thought on *Sein* a knowledge of a philosophical nature? Does he proceed as a true philosopher in suggesting a thought on *Sein* isolated from logic and metaphysics, and, even more, in having enunciated such a thought by means of a constant belligerence against these philosophical sciences? The answer was provided by Saint Justin of Samaria many centuries before Heidegger immersed himself in his search for a non-philosophical or extra-metaphysical thought on *Sein*. This martyr philosopher long ago reminded us that our civilization, because of the arbitrariness of human language, assigns indistinctly the name of φιλόσοφοι both to those who established the truth of things in respecting strictly the rules of philosophy and, though now improperly, to those who moved away from such a truth after scorning the immutable principles of rigorous philosophical knowledge.[17] As with many other thinkers now legion in the Modern Age, Heidegger must then be considered a philosopher, at least according to these teachings of St. Justin.

Consequently, the Heideggerian revolution of philosophy cannot avoid paying the burdensome price for a thought that tried to build a new philosophy on the basis of a rejection of philosophy itself. In this sense, insofar as it has been built with a patent animadversion against the principles and the conclusions of metaphysics, Heideggerian thought on being does not belong to the genus of the philosophical knowledge inaugurated in the pre-Christian age by the philosophers and also by the φυσιολόγοι who lived before Socrates. At most, Heidegger's thought on *Sein* goes back to Parmenides' incipient pre-scientific thought, not as a retrieval of the master of Elea's speculation – whose merits are excessively exaggerated nowadays simply because he was a remote forerunner of univocist monism – but as an exegetical exaltation, inspired by Hegel's system, intended to throw into relief the kernel of the modern principle of immanence sketched prematurely in the remaining fragments of the poem Περὶ φύσεως of the chief of the Eleatic school.

It is likely that few will be satisfied with our assessment of Heideggerian thought on *Sein*. It would be easy to contradict it with texts from Heidegger and even with many interpretations given by authors who disagree with what is held here.

---

17   Cf. Saint Justin the Martyr, *Apol. I*, ch. 4: PG 6,332–33; ch. 7: PG 6,337, and ch. 26: PG 6,369. See M. E. Sacchi, *El espíritu filosófico y la exaltación de la verdad* (Buenos Aires: Ediciones de la Universidad Católica Argentina, 1996), pp. 44–45.

But the insoluble confusion into which such interpretations of Heidegger's theories lead arises directly from the waverings, obscurities, and ambiguities that mark the inextricable style chosen by the German philosopher when he presented his personal thought, to such an extent that from time to time some fall into the malicious temptation of suspecting that he had intended for it to be unintelligible. Nevertheless, even excluding this evil intention, the analysis of Heidegger's thought confirms step by step his remoteness from the lineage of genuine philosophers. Whereas these philosophers have always believed that human reason is ordered naturally to the understanding of the most diaphanous witnesses of the truth of things that are, Heidegger seemed to have reckoned that the ordering of man toward truth would require that he develops a deliberately entangled thought. It is not a sheer coincidence that the investigation of the Heideggerian thought on *Sein* needs a philological-notional surgery that purifies it of its whimsically abstruse framework, although there is a little prospect of carrying it through to a successful conclusion.

Chapter II

The Heideggerian Arbitration of First Philosophy

Heidegger's death in 1976 left many with the impression that the German philosopher had halted the historical path of metaphysics. His opinions both on the nature of first philosophy and on the vicissitudes of the path traveled by this science from the time of its early manifestations in ancient Greece until today have been received by many as final judgments. According to a widely accepted appraisal, Heidegger was the last censor of metaphysics, a hanging judge whose sentence raised the scaffold on which the science of being as such breathed its last. Not everyone shares this impression, however, since others have sought to overturn the verdict by reversing the terms of the aforementioned position. On this view, Heidegger was the last of the great metaphysicians, someone who harshly criticized the science of common being as it had acquired a certain form in the history of Western thought, but, at the same time, inaugurated a new age of first philosophy, having purified it of all the vices acquired during its troubled development over the centuries.

Despite their disagreement, these interpretations of Heidegger's intervention in the so-called *problem of metaphysics* have a common denominator, for they recognize that the Fribourg philosopher effectively divided the history of our science into a prior and a posterior period defined by his involvement in the matter. Some think that Heidegger eliminated forever the possibility of metaphysics; others suggest that, after Heidegger, metaphysics is only possible insofar as it conforms to the schema of the new thought about *Sein* propounded by Heidegger in the texts that he published throughout his long literary career. What place does metaphysics have in Heidegger's thought?

One can observe that both positions show a common defect, viz. their unjustified agreement with the Heideggerian attitude about metaphysics. Both camps submit the fortunes of first philosophy to an authority – Heidegger's thought – without providing any philosophical basis for doing so. His thought would indeed be authoritative for elucidating the question of whether the science of being as such has the character of a knowledge worthy of the task that it has been assigned historically, and above all, the task of furnishing a suitable knowledge of *Sein*.

But why has authority been given to Heideggerian thought to arbitrate the dispute about the philosophical competence of metaphysics, particularly the efficacy of this science to deal with *Sein* itself? Some think that there is only one answer to such a question: other than being the last word in this subject, Heidegger's thought on the science of being in common and also about *Sein* is taken to be an unimpeachable authority. Why? The reason this *potestas suprema* is based on three unfounded assumptions: First, that Heidegger described comprehensively and accurately the history of Western metaphysics' errors; second, that his criticism of this radically flawed metaphysics is overwhelming and irrefutable; third, that Heidegger organized a thought on *Sein* that not only surmounts the failure imputed to first philosophy, but also substitutes for metaphysics the only kind of thought about *Sein* sufficiently able to make known what *Sein* itself is. This obsequiousness is prompted by feeling and emotion, motives alien to the genuine spirit of philosophy. It is a servile acquiescence to the critique of metaphysics contained in Heideggerian thought about *Sein* which is unsupported by any examination of the proper nature of the science of being as such and merely stipulates the truth of what Heidegger said about the history and epistemic organization of first philosophy.

Our aim is not to examine Heidegger's texts concerning the history and the essence of metaphysics with a view to verifying whether the above-mentioned interpretations of his thought are faithful or not to his personal opinions. We believe that the agitation and controversies stirred up by the German philosopher's statements about the so-called *problem of metaphysics* must be considered *ab ovo* despite his declarations as well as his noteworthy and eloquent silences on this matter. To be exact, it is necessary to reverse the terms on which this debate has been carried out hitherto. However scandalous it may sound to those who remain firm in praising the much-acclaimed Heideggerian revolution of metaphysics, we think that there are no acceptable philosophical reasons to subject the integrity and the fortune of this science to the judgment of a single thinker, whoever he may be.

In contrast to what happens in other classes of scientific knowledge obtainable by the human mind – for example, in sacred theology–, philosophy is not acquired by recourse to any authority; not because there are few philosophers endowed with a genuine philosophical authority, but because the analytic that the philosophizing intellect must respect does not take into account the authority of these philosophers as an efficacious reason for demonstrating conclusions. It is worthwhile to recall a famous remark of St. Thomas Aquinas on this matter: Whereas arguments from authority which are based on the inerrancy of divine revelation have the greatest efficacy in demonstrative inferences in sacred theology, arguments supported merely by human reason, whose frailty is patent, are manifestly feeble.[1] In short: although there is no problem with the wonder and gratitude we feel for the scientific achievements of the great masters of philosophy, such gratitude and wonder provides no warrant for canonizing such a science and even less the philosophers who by their achievements contributed to human wisdom.

First philosophy clearly cannot tolerate that truths which are attained by metaphysicians' apodictic reasoning, the very truths of which it properly consists, be dragged into an inquisitorial court governed by the teaching of an author who has arrogated to himself the prerogative of judging them and granting either a *placet* or condemnation on the assumption of the competence of extra-metaphysical thinking. Metaphysics does not admit the existence of any *problem of metaphysics*; much less that its intrinsic consistency is subject to the fictional aporia that it must solve the question concerning 'Heidegger and the problem of metaphysics,' as if the solution to this question were a *conditio sine qua non* for the restoration of its allegedly broken health, or the decree of its eventual extinction. The epistemic primacy of metaphysics did not in the past suffer any intrinsic harm from the onslaughts of Ockham, Luther, Descartes, Hume, Kant, Hegel, and Wittgenstein, to name a few of its more strenuous distorters and detractors. No more is Heidegger justified in setting himself up as an arbiter to determine the failure or success of the science of being as such.

In the face of this insolent arbitrator, metaphysics tenaciously resists the Heideggerian attempt to confute it since its own theorems are absolutely certain and its epistemic consistency invulnerable. But first philosophy has another reason to reject the criticism advanced against it by Heidegger. Not only has he never demonstrated that the science of being as such has failed to know the act of being, for it is precisely such

---

1   "Licet locus ab auctoritate quae fundatur super ratione humana, sit infirmissimus; locus tamen ab auctoritate quae fundatur super revelatione divina, est efficacissimus" (*Summ. theol.* I q. 1 a. 8 ad 2um).

knowledge insofar as it is the science of that which is thanks to this act, but he has also never successfully shown that there is a thinking about *Sein* which does not coincide with metaphysical knowledge of things that are. There should be no surprise since everything is thanks to the act of being that makes it be, or that entifies it by making it a being.

Like many other modern thinkers, Heidegger is uneasy with the ἀπόδειξις of scientific reason for understanding things by way of analytic argument. The Fribourg thinker also believed that philosophy can abandon the logical force of demonstrative discourse and become merely a thought limited to declaring what thought itself is without bringing forth any argument in which conclusions, the object of epistemic knowledge, depend on the premises in which they are virtually contained. This non-scientific style adopted by many modern thinkers raises a serious doubt: To what extent is it possible to dub philosophical a thinking divorced from the syllogistic method, which is indispensable for true epistemic knowledge, which has sunk to the infra-philosophical level of opinion devoid of every apodictic support? Does the philosopher's task consist of just thinking and saying what is thought rather than of deducing truth through the reasoning why that demonstratively reaches a *cognitio certa per causas*? How then could we distinguish philosophy from a hybrid logomachy, from an anodyne sport, or from entertaining ramblings, even though they are sometimes adorned with the meager dignity of elegance?

Let us recognize Heidegger's responsibility for the arbitration aimed at settling the so-called *problem of metaphysics* which, despite his prior criticism of first philosophy, many authors assign to him. Heidegger repeatedly stated his personal standpoint on this matter by trying to fulfill a philosophical task independently of whether the results of his thinking in that respect did or did not agree with the truth. However, strictly speaking, this arbitration of metaphysics is a device employed by many admirers of Heidegger who seek to extend his thought, but who at the same time show a regrettable obsequiousness, ingenuously yielding to his doctrine and rejecting without foundation all the metaphysical theories that he had previously discarded. Nevertheless, this suggests ignorance both of the essence of the science of being as such and of the logical rules that must govern any consideration of its true nature. Thus, it is not a simple reiteration of the errors Heidegger fell into when others perpetuate their own position on the nature and the history of first philosophy; it takes it further into a flagrant sectarianism dedicated to eliminating metaphysics, or rather something so called, through the promotion of Heideggerian thought about *Sein* as its suitable substitute.

This attempt can be summarized as follows: metaphysics has disappointed the human vocation to think about *Sein;* consequently, authentic thought about *Sein* demands that we leave metaphysics behind because both its internal failure and its prolonged history of neglecting the *Sein* concealed in being. Now, since Heidegger's thought would be the optimal substitute for first philosophy, he must be seen as someone who would play the role of a genuine *discoverer* of the truth of *Sein,* i.e., a truth hidden throughout history that had to wait for Heidegger's appearance on the twentieth-century philosophical scene before men noticed it for the first time.

These nonsensical claims of his help us understand why Heideggerian thought is being reinterpreted in a novel way. According to this new interpretation, he was not just one among the many contemporary philosophers interested in restoring the fundamental outlines of the theory of the act of being in the philosophical panorama, but someone who propounded a theory of *Sein* that, apart from its differences from the conception of philosophy held in the framework of Western culture, evidences a curious relationship with a thought bearing the mark of religion, or at least something close to religion.

Moreover, bearing in mind that Heideggerian thought is praised, exploited, and promoted by his acolytes in this direction, one can see why some interpreters of Heidegger suspect that his thinking about *Sein* contains a certain dose of gnostic esoterism which is extremely difficult to describe. But how far may we justifiably extend this suspicion of a gnostic esoterism in Heidegger's thinking about *Sein* in Heidegger? His disciples repeatedly describe him as an *alter Parmenides*, a thinker whose speculative freshness would have adorned the philosophy of Socrates' predecessors. He is hailed as the founder of a thought about *Sein* that will overcome its unfortunate neglect in a metaphysics incapable of disclosing its truth which is hidden in the objective darkness of being. The now-increasing recognition of the esoteric gnosis that infiltrated Heideggerian thinking was already manifest to some philosophers at the time *Sein und Zeit* was published in 1927. There are not, however, many studies on this aspect of Heidegger's thinking, but it has been noted in some lesser known studies. In 1932, Julius Kraft, who studied with Leonard Nelson at Göttingen and Franz Oppenheimer at Frankfurt, published a book in which he bitterly attacked the phenomenology of Husserl and his disciples, above all, Max Scheler's. Kraft's anti-phenomenological attack was also directed at Heidegger as one who, in following the footsteps of Husserl, planned a philosophy in the manner of a "cosmic event" that would bring about a leap into mystical thinking. This mystical thinking consists of an esoteric style of thinking that Kraft relates to concerns evident in the spirit of the young Heidegger before his self-imposed eleven years literary silence between 1916 and 1927, that is, from the publication of his university monograph *Die Kategorien- und Bedeutungslehre des Duns Scotus* until the appearance of *Sein und Zeit* in the *Jahrbuch für Phänomenologie und phänomenologische Forschung*, edited by Husserl.[2]

---

2   Cf. J. Kraft, *Von Husserl zu Heidegger: Kritik der phänomenologischen Philosophie*, 2nd ed. (Frankfurt am Main: Verlag "Öffentliches Leben," 1957), p. 83. See also pp. 83–104. Kraft's position was shared later by W. Hoeres, *Kritik der transzendental-philosophischen Erkenntnistheorie* (Stuttgart, Berlin, Köln & Mainz: W. Kohlhammer Verlag, 1969), p. 85.

Some years later, with no less ardor than Kraft, Helmut Kuhn noted that in Heidegger's work there are certain inklings that both set him off from the Western philosophical tradition, and cause one to question the philosophical character of such thinking whose light comes in the darkness of a crisis of despair.[3] Kuhn was of the opinion that in *Sein und Zeit* Heidegger had left behind the philosophical principles held by Søren Kierkegaard. If Heidegger had observed these principles circumspectly, he would have remained in touch with the oldest tradition of philosophy. Since the publication of *Sein und Zeit*, he stressed the existential value of anguish as a regression to a pagan eschatology derived from Hölderlin's poetic works. In doing so, Heidegger was moved by his affection for certain trends that he found in the no less pagan mentality of some pre-Socratic philosophers.[4]

According to Kuhn, the influence of Hölderlin's neopaganism on the formation of Heidegger's thought was decisive, especially in the poet's exaltation of ancient Greek pantheism: in those happy days of Greece, the gods mingled with men, but then Christ, the "last of the Olympians," arrived, and the tragedy could not be controlled. The heavens drew away from the earth, the temples tumbled down, desolation reached the altars, men began to suffer with the cold of silence, and, starting from these tribulations, mankind waits grievingly for gods' return to this worldly landscape. Once in the grips of Hölderlin's messianic prophesy, Kuhn wrote, Heidegger wanted to eliminate from his thought the metaphysical language that would impede his thinking about *Sein* as he sought to regain the purity of pre-Socratic paganism lost for two millennia in the philosophical reign of Plato and Aristotle. In accepting Hölderlin's authority, Kuhn says, Heidegger awaited anxiously the return of the "absent God."

3   Cf. H. Kuhn, *Begegnung mit dem Nichts: Ein Versuch über die Existenzphilosophie* (Tübingen: Verlag J. C. B. Mohr [Paul Siebeck], 1950), p. 137.

4   Cf. *ibid.*, p. 153.

But, how would he have recognized the expected God? Kuhn's judgment is categorical: Heidegger's works give no assurance that he knew the difference between the divine and the demoniac.[5]

Those who consider Kuhn's statements carefully can understand that he was pointing toward an even more serious problem in the background of Heidegger's thought. Indeed, Kuhn noted that Heideggerian thought contains an unimaginable perspective. Post-Socratic philosophy, the great Western philosophy, with Plato and Aristotle in the lead, according to Heidegger, arose and developed by means of a perfidious break with the sources of the earliest philosophical thinking that came about with the work of Parmenides, Heraclitus, and Anaximander. Heidegger believed that the philosophy illumined by the principles of Plato and Aristotle ostracized true philosophical thought. Moreover, since it was in this current of philosophy that Christianity found an ally, the hopeful impulse of pagan innocence was left behind as the dawn of philosophical purity was ruined with the proclamation of Jesus of Nazareth. In short, Kuhn realized that Heidegger absorbed the marrow of Hölderlin's neopagan mysticism. In following Hölderlin, the Fribourg philosopher asserted that the crisis of Western philosophy, mainly of metaphysical knowledge, arose from the combination of the three dominant currents of thought of the past twenty-four centuries: Platonism, Aristotelianism, and Christianity. This crisis resulted in the subsequent abolition of the pagan spirit, a spirit defeated both by syllogistic reasoning and supernatural faith in a God who is neither something of this world nor an idol of the Gentiles.

Because many philosophers today reject the suspicion of a gnostic esoterism in Heidegger's thinking about *Sein*, it is necessary to emphasize the two features of this thinking that occasioned this suspicion. One of them is extrinsic to

---

5   Cf. *ibid.*, p. 159.

Heidegger's works, namely the broad reception of his proposal to substitute for metaphysics a thinking about *Sein*. His
followers attributed to him not only the typical physiognomy
of a discoverer, but even of a *redeemer* of *Sein* because he
repaired the concealment that it suffered in the history of the
science of being as such, by speculating on the purity of its
extra-entitative truth and setting up that thinking about *Sein*
as a human thought free from the metaphysical failures that
obstinately consigned it to oblivion. The other feature where
Heidegger tried to emend the supposed failure of Western
metaphysics in its endeavor to think about *Sein*. That is why
he expressly claimed that *Sein* would be dependent on man
or, more precisely still, on the *Dasein*, or human existent,
through the famous anxiety or care (*Sorge*) outlined in the
pages of *Sein und Zeit*.[6] If this were so, the Heideggerian
image of the human being would reflect an extraordinary
nearness to that of a *conditor* of the act of being, as someone
who has the "care" of *Sein* in his charge, someone who acts as
its "shepherd." This would silence those who want to place
Heidegger's thought about *Sein* in a field completely separated from any religious or mythical lucubration.

The suspicion of this crypto-mystical direction in
Heideggerian thought about *Sein* is also shared by Leszek
Kolakowski. In his analysis of the relations of *Sein* and language existing in that thought, the Polish philosopher noted
the old tradition of belief in a close relation between man's
words and knowledge of the inner essence of the things they
signify. But just as philosophy proved the arbitrary and con-
ventional condition of human language – in this respect
Kolakowski admits the semantic theory developed by
Aristotle and St. Thomas Aquinas –, so we can also detect the
survival of the old mythical illusion that yearns to find in

---

6   Cf. *Sein und Zeit*, 11th ed. (Tübingen: Max Niemeyer, 1967), Part One,
     Chap. 6: "Die Sorge als Seins des Daseins," pp. 180–230; and Part Two,
     Chap. 3: "Die Ganze inkönnen des Daseins und die Zeitlichkeit als der
     ontologische Sinn der Sorge," pp. 301–33.

linguistic signs the names the gods have imposed on things, even more, their own heavenly names. Kolakowski indicates that this mythical tradition persists in magic, in many religious rites, in cabalistic rumination, in the entire spectrum of esoterism, and in some conceptions of sacred language. But contemporary philosophy, according to Kolakowski, also yielded to the temptation of absorbing this mystification of the meaning of human words. A clear example of such a temptation is found in Heidegger's work, for he maintained the illusory possibility of a knowledge about the signification of words that would include an immediate grasp of the essence of what they signify. This would be possible because things have sprung up or come into being endowed with their own names, that is to say with the same names whose semantic message would enable to us to understand the core of their quiddities.[7]

Therefore, the alleged Heideggerian overcoming of metaphysics leads to the limit of human understanding. Once having excluded the competence of the science of being as such to deal with *Sein*, it is necessary to ask if philosophy still retains any suitability for satisfying the human vocation to know the things that are and the act of being by which they are. In facing this question, Heidegger and his followers brandish some rhetorical arguments, often excessively adorned with a bouquet of aesthetic accessories, by which, although only momentarily, they elude the debate about the query underlying this intricate mental process: Can human reason obtain a knowledge of *Sein* that claims to be of a formal

---

7   "When Heidegger says *'die Sprache spricht'* . . . or *'Die Sprache ist das Haus des Seins'* . . . , what he apparently means is both that one can arrive at a knowledge of the genuine meaning of words and so penetrate into the essence of things (which he repeatedly tried to do in analysing the Greek and German roots of the philosophical vocabulary), and that things are born together with their names" (L. Kolakowski, *Religion: If There Is No God . . . On God, the Evil, Sin and Other Worries of the So-called Philosophy of Religion* [London: Fontana Press, 1982; South Bend, Ind.: St. Augustine's Press, 2001], p. 184).

philosophical nature and beyond metaphysical understanding? The Heideggerian answer to this question is well known: man is capable of thinking about *Sein* as such, but first philosophy, on the contrary, is incapable of thinking about it as pure *Sein* because the authentic thought about *Sein*, in the last analysis, would differ utterly from metaphysics. Even more, first philosophy and the thought about *Sein* could not coincide because they are separated by an irremediable equivocity, to such an extent that Heidegger contended that they are destined to clash with each other. That is why he said that insofar as we think as metaphysicians do, we are not thinking properly.[8] First philosophy would not belong to the range of thought, at least of that thought to which the apprehension of *Sein* is reserved; rather it would be as an adolescent stage of thought prior to the adult age indispensable for thinking about *Sein*. But how might one understand this paradox of a metaphysical thinking which would be at odds with thinking itself without first determining what the proper nature of the science of being as such is?

Once he has declared the incomprehensible contradiction of asserting that the act of thinking is not the act of thinking – as we just saw, Heidegger stated that whoever thinks as the first philosopher does would not be thinking –, he declared that it is essential to metaphysical thinking to remain in an attitude that would exclude thinking itself. The science of being as such left unthought something of the essence of *Sein*, but what metaphysicians have not thought is the very basis on which their thought is supported. Surprisingly, according to Heidegger, this not-thinking about that which is forgotten of *Sein*, is not a defect of metaphysics.[9] But how could a science base its argumentation on something that, insofar as unthought, would be unknown to human reason? Is it the same thing as saying that science, the true intellectual

---

8   Cf. *Was heißt Denken?*, p. 40.

9   Cf. *ibid.*, p. 42.

knowledge of things, is based on ignorance and, on the other hand, that we would think about *Sein* once we discarded the science of those things entified by the act of being itself?

Heidegger stated frequently that the supreme feat of the human spirit consists in thinking about *Sein*. In his opinion, metaphysics does not satisfy this highest desire of our mind because it cast *Sein* historically and systematically into an oblivion that kept it out of man's understanding. The thought about *Sein* must be exercised regardless of every attempt to trace it back to the speculative channels of the science of being as such. Therefore, it is time to inquire if the challenge of metaphysics posed by Heideggerian thought about *Sein*, and by those who echoed it as well, has any philosophical justification.

Since the publication of *Sein und Zeit* in 1927, Heidegger has expounded his thought about *Sein* behind a veil of an exotic linguistic apparatus. Why did he expound it so, scorning the language philosophers used throughout centuries? It is true that the words of human language, without excluding philosophical terms, signify *ad placitum*. It is also true that the meaning of many philosophical terms underwent alterations through the ages, sometimes important ones. However, the Heideggerian invention of a new lexicography has not been limited to a mere alteration of the nominal signification of numerous words, but arose as a consequence of two prior difficulties. On the one hand, Heidegger cast aside many concepts, aporiae, and philosophical inferences because he could not adapt them to his own thought on *Sein*, and after that he also cast aside the language once used to express something that, in his opinion, could be called *residual philosophy* or maybe *philosophical undercurrent*. On the other hand, Heidegger sketched new problems to replace that discarded philosophy and to raise another through an alternative semantics, one very different from that already cast away.

Why this notional and nominal metamorphosis whose usefulness and success neither Heidegger nor anyone else could either calculate or guarantee? Even more, why would another philosophy be necessary once the failure of philosophy itself was asserted? What remedy could amend the collapse of philosophy, especially the collapse of its noblest science, i.e., metaphysics, a science which supposedly had become exhausted because of its impotence to deal with a *Sein* that this very science itself had condemned to a shameful oblivion? Heidegger did not hesitate: philosophy, particularly first philosophy, would need to be radically overcome by means of a *thought*, of a meta-philosophical and trans-metaphysical *Denken*, destined to accomplish in the human spirit a reciprocal and inseparable consubstantiation of thought and *Sein*. That is why Heidegger believed that to be and to think would be the same thing, just as his mentors Parmenides and Hegel had before him. To think would be to think about the thinkable *Sein* and also the thought *Sein*; to be would be the thinkable *Sein* and also to be thought by thought itself. Hence, the original unity, the deepest arcanum of everything, the insurmountable, the primeval, and unifying redoubt of multiplicity, the wholeness of the absolute, and the essence of the very foundation (*Grund*).

Heideggerian thought about *Sein* has been developed as an attempt to surpass philosophy, mainly metaphysics. This thought aimed at defeating the science of being as such by punishing its sinful oblivion of *Sein*. This thought has both a retaliatory and supplementary thrust, for the emptiness caused by the metaphysical oblivion of *Sein* would be filled by the only substitute with which *Sein* maintains something more than a circumstantial affinity – thought itself. With this aim in view, thought would not be limited to a critique of traditional Western philosophy; it also would need to defy strenuously the prototypical manifestation of the failure of this philosophy, viz. metaphysics, a science unsuitable for thinking *Sein* as a pure *Sein* because of its restriction to a speculation about being as such, or about something that is not *Sein* itself, for the knowledge of *Sein* would only be within the reach of that thought insofar as it overcomes the oblivion to which first philosophy condemned it.

The challenge to metaphysics put forth by Heideggerian thought about *Sein* is founded on the attribution of a supraphilosophical greatness to the latter. Heidegger believed that his thought about *Sein* would exceed and remedy the failure of metaphysics because the truth about *Sein* would have awaited patiently for its liberation from first philosophy. Once it becomes free from this nugatory science, which would not allow *Sein* to escape from its concealment in being, the truth about *Sein* would disclose itself to man's thought, which is capable of effecting and appreciating the epiphany of *Sein* in spite of a philosophy insensitive or indifferent to everything that surpasses the darkness of being as such where it would remain hidden and forgotten.

Thought would rise to the truth of *Sein* by defeating and exceeding a philosophy that had neither known, nor wished to go beyond, the limits of being. Metaphysicians had speculated about being as such in making use of a λόγος restricted to scanning the objectivity of the ὄν, but the truth of *Sein* exceeds the intelligibility of being. The *horizon* of Sein would surpass the objectivity of being and would escape from metaphysical understanding, which dealt with its subject by confining its philosophical theorization to the intelligibility of being as such, attainable through the methods of logic. Moreover, the truth of *Sein* would not be attained by metaphysical means, whose method is the analytical speculation of epistemic reason, but by means of the reciprocal impregnation of consciousness and of that truth acted by a thought which would keep them joined in their original unity. Again, to be and to think would be the same thing, as Parmenides and Hegel previously proposed.

The thought about *Sein* refuses to grow weak in a reiteration of the historical death throes of metaphysics that would lead philosophy to fall into the oblivion of *Sein* with all that ensued, that is to say that metaphysics would be both the idolatry of being as such and the apostasy of the Western spirit insofar as it would have desisted from thinking about *Sein* as pure *Sein*. So, the transition from μυ'θος to λόγος – the move that gave rise to Western philosophy – would have come to an end with the downfall of metaphysics, which happened many centuries later in our own time when Nietzsche reviled the philosophical tradition and the Christian religion. This consequence should lead us to look elsewhere for an entry into the truth of *Sein*, i.e., through a passage from a disappointing ἐπιστήμη to a previously delogicized *Denken*, which is the only way to think *Sein* independently of the things whose objectivity obstructs its idyll with a consciousness destined entirely to think about itself, in the same way that, also entirely, *Sein* itself would be destined to be thought by the very thought of which such a conscience consists.

Heidegger outlined this singular thought about *Sein* once his arbitration of the pseudo-problem of metaphysics persuaded him that it was nonsense to go on having hope in a philosophical speculation on *Sein* given the miscarried historical evolution of the science of being as being ordered to such end.

Chapter III

The Rejection of Metaphysics as Ontotheology

When dealing with the so-called *problem of metaphysics*, Heidegger sought inspiration in the same principles that had induced Kant to write the *Critique of Pure Reason* in the eighteenth century. Even more, in following Kant, the Heideggerian description of first philosophy as ontotheology implies that it is a discipline whose discursive research (λόγος) is focused on the knowledge of being (ὄν) whose supreme manifestation would be God, the divine entity (θεός). But this Kantian description of ontotheology, which Heidegger submissively accepted, does not go beyond a mere nominal approach to the meaning of metaphysical theorizing and the range of topics considered in its argumentative development, for in sketching ontotheology Kant assigned it a bias that must be remembered, for he distinguishes ontotheology from what he called *cosmotheology*. Whereas the latter would deduce the existence of an *original essence* by means of the data of general experience, although without any inquiry into things existing in the outside world, the former would try to know that original essence independently of all

empirical apprehension, that is by deducing it only from the
content of the concepts of the human mind.[1]

The importance of the Kantian schema of ontotheology
does not lie in a clarification of etymology meant to shed light
on the nature of metaphysics, but in the fact that this science,
as ontotheology, is said to be impossible. Speculative reason
allegedly lacks the perceptive power sufficient to know the
things existing beyond the consciousness of the knowing subject and, consequently, it can neither demonstrate that those
things or God Himself are, even less what they are. In short,
as an ontotheology developed by theoretical reason, first philosophy is accused of being a wasted knowledge because of
its inability to infer anything about outside things – God
Himself among them –, which cannot be known due to the
supposed impotence of that reason to analyze any object that
is not *a priori* immanent to subjective consciousness.
Therefore, according to its Kantian definition, ontotheology
implies the impossibility of metaphysics as knowledge of
speculative reason.

Heidegger adopted this version of metaphysics as
ontotheology without having noticed that Kant's thesis is
damaged by an intrinsic contradiction, for it does not make
any sense to assert that metaphysics is ontotheology – a discourse about both being and God – and at the same time to
deny the possibility of a knowledge of the extra-subjective
world and of a deity extrinsic to the knowing subject. Indeed,
the mere affirmation of a human λόγος that can know something of being and of God implies that the intellect of the
rational animal is endowed with a potency capable of dealing
with things different from its own subjectivity. This is why the
Kantian-Heideggerian consideration of metaphysics as
ontotheology and the denial of the scientific status of first philosophy stand in contradiction to each other. Furthermore,

---

1   Cf. I. Kant, *Kritik der reinen Vernunft*, B 660, ed. by B. Erdmann, in *Kants
     gesammelte Schriften*, ed. by the Royal Prussian Academy of Sciences
     [Berlin: Reimer, 1904], vol. III, p. 420.

they require that the scope of man's knowledge be confined to the range immanent to the consciousness of the one exercising it. Therefore, it must be admitted that this key thesis of Kant's agnosticism, later compliantly received in Heidegger's works from the publication of *Sein und Zeit*, entails a submissiveness to the immanentist ferment on which it depends and to which it is joined essentially.

This very conception of ontotheology, or of first philosophy itself, is included in Heidegger's schema of a new thought about *Sein*. If metaphysics has an ontotheological constitution, such as described above, its sad fate as a failed science would not differ from that which Kant anticipated in the *Critique of Pure Reason*. The transcendental critique of knowledge came to an inexorable result, for, not being able to capture anything from the outside world or from things themselves, the object of speculative reason must always coincide with something immanent to consciousness, i.e., with thought itself.

Once this sketch that excludes metaphysics from the *arbor scientiarum* is adopted, Heidegger also admitted Kant's opinion which holds the absolute primacy of consciousness, as may be understood from a reading of the text where he explained his views on the ontotheological constitution attributed to the science of being as such. Thought, he says, contains something inherent to itself insofar as its intrinsic questionableness drives it to be concerned with this immanent thing which once thought by thought itself, would revert thought to itself.[2] But if this Heideggerian theory leads one to ask what is this thing intrinsic to thought – a thing seemingly endowed with the power necessary to raise a questionableness that requires it to think about itself in its own immanence to consciousness –, it also leads one to ask to what extent that

---

2   "Die Sache des Denkens bedrängt das Denken in der Weise, daß sie das Denken erst zu einer Sache und von dieser her zu ihm selbst bringt" ("Die onto-theo-logische Verfassung der Metaphysik," in *Identität und Differenz* [Pfullingen: Günther Neske, 1957], p. 37).

thing and that questionableness inhere in consciousness without any relation to an external object. Thus, Heidegger's propositions seem to indicate that thought is compelled to face this questionableness as something whose immanence to the knowing consciousness does not differ at all from a true *res subsistens* because its lack of reference with respect to the things that are *ad extra*, in the external world, allows it to exist with thought independently of any causality proceeding from outside the consciousness: thought itself effects it in the thinking mind.

The adoption of Kant's condemnation of metaphysics as ontotheology prompted Heidegger to bestow on thought the aforementioned absolute primacy with respect to things existing in the outside world. That is why thought would also have an absolute primacy with respect to *Sein* itself, unless they do not differ at all from each other, but are the same thing. In any case, Heidegger believed that thought, by concerning itself with itself, was forced to face a questionableness that would inhere in its own entity as true thought, and even in *Sein* as thought by thought itself. But what gives rise to this questionableness supposedly intrinsic to thought itself without any reference to things foreign to its knowing entity? Whence does the questionableness perceived by thought in its own intimacy come into thought itself? Heidegger did not answer this question, one that reiterates basically the same schema that once encouraged Descartes to postulate the *cogito* as something that would precede the act of being as the very starting point of the life of the spirit.

The Heideggerian regression to the principle dear to modern idealism may be seen in the immediate redundancy of ontological immanentism summed up in the thesis according to which man would think by thinking his own thought. Thought itself would be the redoubt of its intrinsic questionableness in man's very intimacy. Now, on the one hand, this theory tacitly asserts the subsistence of thought as exercised by a human being, such that the rational animal would exercise it as a perpetual act, for our thought would achieve its own entity without need of any causal influence from things existing in the outside world. So Heidegger agrees fully with Kant's agnostic position, which granted to consciousness both an entitative and an operative autonomy independent of any object outside man's soul. On the other hand, like Descartes, Heidegger had to say that the first and primordial connection of thought with *Sein* would occur insofar as *Sein* itself inheres in human consciousness, because thought allegedly finds it by grasping the questionableness of which thought itself would consist – *a nosse ad esse valet consequentia*. *Sein*, therefore, is not the act that makes every thing in the universe to be; nor, moreover, does our intellect know through speculation on beings that such an act makes them be and be what they are. On the contrary, *Sein* is said to be a sort of reflection of a thought that permanently demands the dialogical presence of an affable companion of its own lineage and, moreover, one that is capable of consoling thought itself in the solitary existence that it is obliged to suffer once emancipated from the objectivity of extra-mental things.

Therefore, not being the act of that which exists outside man's soul, *Sein*, in the end, cannot avoid being the very act of a consciousness that put it *a priori* at the disposal of the thought of which it would consist. That is why Heidegger coherently accepted and followed the path of idealism which began when Descartes, in his *Discourse on Method*, enunciated the motto *Je pense, donc je suis*, a motto later explicitly restored by Kant in the *Critique of Pure Reason* as he asserted the transcendental constitution of objects. Hegel admitted it subsequently as the key of his pantheistic system, where there is no possibility of destroying the compact dialectical identity of reality and idea, of history and spirit, of logic and metaphysics, of the act of being and nothingness, and, at last, of the world and God.

The Hegelian system is not mentioned superfluously. Heidegger's lecture "The Ontotheological Constitution of Metaphysics," which dates from 1957 and was delivered more extensively in a seminar given shortly before in Todtnauberg, involves several remarks on Hegel's *Science of Logic*.[3] In that lecture Heidegger clarified his position in relation to the questions posed above, among which it is necessary to throw into relief the confession that his exegesis of thought, especially in the plenitude that it would reach as a thought about that which is thought, must be understood in the light of the essence of the transcendental that Kant sketched in the *Critique of Pure Reason*.[4] This fundamental confession of Heidegger's discloses both the deepest aim of his critique of metaphysics and, at the same time, the scope he assigned to the thought about *Sein* that would act as a substitute for the Western scientific tradition's first philosophy. Indeed, Heidegger's confession includes three relevant aspects of his doctrine. First, his consideration of thought does not consist of a philosophical analysis of this act, but on an *exegesis*, which, according to the entitative perfection he attributes to thought, is not limited to a mere interpretative function, but contains an exaltation of and even an apology for it as well. Second, thought is complete as thought about thought, or as a thought about thought that thinks itself. Third, the plenitude of this thinking about something thought by thought itself in its immanence to consciousness is identified with the very same transcendental of Kant's *Critique of Pure Reason*, i.e., with a construction of objects through an anticipation of forms *a priori* which would lie in mind independently of any relation to things of the outside world and other than the knowing subject. In short, Heidegger echoes the transcendental schema developed previously by Kant, which is the indispensable antecedent of Hegel's pantheistic

---

3 Cf. *Identität und Differenz*, preface, p. 9.
4 Cf. *ibid.*, p. 38.

system, even if the latter did not admit several aspects of that Kantian transcendental schema.

Nevertheless, Heidegger says that, in thinking itself, thought stumbles on *Sein*. This *Sein* is claimed to exceed all the things that together had historically engaged the concerns of Western metaphysics.[5] But it implies that thought, even though *Sein* had been its preeminent concern among all other things, does not leave behind its devotion to thought itself. This devotion warrants its fidelity to the very entity of thinking, which includes the aforementioned questionableness among its attributes.[6] So to speak, thought about thinking would be a thought about the *Sein* thought by thought itself within the range of a consciousness in which that questionableness, which is intrinsic to the knowing entity, lies.

However, it is symptomatic that Heidegger had assigned to thought the task of thinking about *Sein*, since such a thought depends on a questionableness intrinsic to its own entity, for this questionableness oddly enough does not derive from difficulties that can hinder or impede human knowledge of outside things. But if there were no difficulty about exercising thought as the act by which *Sein* is thought in its immanence to thought itself, at least insofar as it becomes isolated and unconcerned with outside things, why would thought be involved in such a questionableness? What questionableness could affect a thought existing in a perpetual act wherein *Sein* would enjoy a place suitable to its character as something essentially constituted to be thought by thought itself? Heidegger's reluctance to answer these questions invites consideration of a possibility that was concealed in his unfortunate indication of a true philosophical problem; namely, has Heidegger, in insisting on the questionableness inherent in thought, particularly to the thought about *Sein* exercised by man, mentioned the true questionableness that

---

5   Cf. *ibid.*
6   Cf. *ibid.*, p. 41.

can happen in the human mode of knowing and the obstacles that can impede the consummation of the understanding of things naturally knowable by our reason?

There are many reasons to pose this question once the nebulous atmosphere that surrounds the Heideggerian postulation of the questionableness of thought is considered, and also to suspect that this supposed questionableness, which Heidegger considered as the problem of thought, is neither a true problem nor even a genuine philosophical one. Instead of a genuine philosophical problem, the so-called Heideggerian *problem* of thought seems rather to hide a conflict of an affective nature arising from his agnostic attitudes. Starting with the publication of *Sein und Zeit* in 1927, Heidegger always attempted to establish why and how thought, enclosed in its self-sufficient immanence to consciousness, thinks about itself while finding within its reach nothing that is not thought or, even better, without being able to intentionally nourish itself from the representative likenesses of any object existing in the outside world. Why? Because a thought about thought itself does not consist of an intentional assimilation of things alien to its own entity, but only of an original unity sustained in a consubstantiality, affinity, sympathy, or identity of thought and of that thought by it. Therefore, the subject of thought, according to Heidegger, is the very thing of which it consists – thought itself –, which allegedly allows it to think about a self-revealed *Sein* that becomes self-evident in the intimacy of thought itself, but by no means in the extra-mental objectivity of things that are.

What has happened to *Sein* in the midst of this conflict which Heidegger believes to be intrinsic to thought? Although Heidegger assigned a problematic character to thought, in fact he ended up showing the typical face of a drama marked by a disordered affectivity, or perhaps made anarchical by the same frustration that overwhelms a thought divorced from the only objects suitable for joining it with the truth of things that are by the act of being. However, this act makes them to be without any human necessity of being thought by any human thought. As immanent to the consciousness that is said to think about it, *Sein* was never considered by Heidegger as an intelligible object or as a correlate of the mind. In his writings *Sein* usually appears as a visitor to consciousness and, at the same time, as something connatural to thought, with which it would have a dialogical relation, simultaneously cordial and troublesome – or rather conflictive –, but above all compensatory for the loneliness that *Sein* would suffer once thought by a mind that had given up understanding it in the only place wherein it would remain free from any human ambition of making it a vassal of consciousness.

Heidegger sketched a thought about *Sein* to replace metaphysics. He adopted this ontological immanentism as a premise of that thought. Once he decided to get to the point, after having patiently essayed many metaphors and rhetorical turns of phrase that constantly hinder any direct and rigorous insight into the heart of things under analysis, the flaws of his judgments on the history of philosophy began to be exposed, with the added difficulty that such opinions were previously elevated to the heights of peremptory and unappealable statements. This is the outstanding case of a question that philosophy can neither give up dealing with nor postpone, viz. the question of the difference between the act of being and being itself.

One of Heidegger's favorite statements is that the difference of *Sein* from being is absent from the history of metaphysics. Nobody, he seems to hold, ever asked about this difference – not even Hegel – until Heidegger himself for the first time retrieved it from its lethargic historical oblivion. Therefore, the disclosure of the difference between being and *Sein*, a difference no one had ever grasped throughout all of the history of philosophy, seems to have been reserved to Heidegger himself.[7] But this opinion is not only at odds with explicit documents from the history of philosophy, and is explainable only by the precarious historiographic information that Heidegger possessed, but it also hides a datum of peculiar connotations which ought to be carefully analyzed by students of his thought, i.e., his self-description as someone who overcame the concealment of *Sein* as something clearly different from being, a truth, he holds, no one had known before himself.

Heidegger was a victim of a misunderstanding caused by his feeble knowledge of the history of philosophy, for the distinction of being and *Sein*, far from having been brought to light by him, had been clearly affirmed long before he called the attention of his twentieth-century colleagues to it.[8] Heidegger's opinions on the history of philosophy have been the object of adulation by his unconditional admirers and, at the same time, of harsh criticisms from his opponents. The latter emphasize that his opinions were destined to favor his own theoretical concerns. They also accuse him of having distorted the meaning of many philosophical theories, especially those of the Greek masters of antiquity and the Schoolmen of the Middle Ages. Moreover, his opinions on modern thought have also earned him justified reproaches, e.g., the just observation that views are confined almost exclusively to a segment of modern German philosophy, since, except for some sporadic quotations of Descartes, Pascal, and a few other authors of different nationality, to all appearances Heidegger was not interested in philosophies developed in other lands. And as if that were not enough, it is very difficult to excuse him for having granted significant philosophical stature to certain authors whose works not only do not

---

7   Cf. *ibid.*, p. 46.

8   Cf. M. E. Sacchi, *La epifanía objetiva del ser* (Buenos Aires: Basileia, 1997), pp. 45–47.

exhibit such importance but, inversely, exude an ostensible antagonism to the most elemental principles of true philosophical knowledge. Let us take some illustrative examples: by what right did Heidegger affirm that Nietzsche's thought represented the *non plus ultra* of Western metaphysics?[9] Is it necessary to remember that Heidegger had recourse to Hölderlin's and Rilke's poems as if they were canonical writings endowed with the virtue of inerrancy? Furthermore, it seems that Heidegger avoided noticing that the assiduous recurrence to the gloomy spirit from which Hölderlin's poetry and Nietzsche's frenetic logomachy arise requires first of all that one remember that their thought, as was attested in testimony from their contemporaries' good sense and medical knowledge, originated and developed in a series of psychosomatic breakdowns which in due course were authoritatively corroborated by physicians as demented episodes. But Heidegger did not discern the philosophical conclusions of a reason rightly rectified by the strength of logic from the thought of writers whose literature is capable of both causing astonishment and provoking delightful sensations, even though it had been hatched in painful states of madness.

Heidegger's opinion on the forgetting of the difference of *Sein* and being is part of those same deficiencies, for we have enough significant examples that attest to an explicit knowledge of that difference in the philosophical tradition. Thus, Aristotle clearly distinguished the act of being of a thing (τὸ εἶναι) and the quiddity that constitutes the nature of the being that exercises such an act (τὸ δὲ τί ἐστιν).[10] Boethius formulated his acclaimed distinction between the act of being (*esse*) and that which is (*id quod est*) in the treatise *De hebdo-*

---

9 Cf. "Nietzsches Wort 'Gott ist tot'" in *Holzwege*, 5th ed. (Frankfurt am Main: Vittorio Klostermann, 1972), pp. 193–247; "Überwindung der Metaphysik," in *Vorträge und Aufsätze*, pp. 75, 77, 79; and "Wer ist Zarathustra?" *Ibid.*, pp. 97–122.

10 Cf. *Analyt. post.* Bk. II, ch. 7: 92 b 10–11.

madibus.[11] We find the clearest exposition of this distinction in St. Thomas Aquinas' metaphysics. The Angelic Doctor said that being – whose first act is the very act of being – is due to this very act and not to what exercises it; hence there is a concrete difference between the being that is and the act of being by which being is a being: "Non sic proprie dicitur quod esse sit, sed quod per esse, aliquid sit."[12] Another example: even though Henry of Ghent was a fierce enemy of Thomism, especially of the famous distinction between the act of being and the essence of creatures, it did not escape him that, ultimately, there is a distinction, at least of reason, between being and the act of being: "Non possum dicere ens et suum esse, licet idem sint in re."[13] Finally, shortly before Heidegger proclaimed that the difference between *Sein* and being had been ignored by preceding philosophy as a whole, a peerless Neo-Thomist work, written during the years of his youthful Neo-scholastic education, was devoted to demonstrate this proposition: "In creaturis itaque *esse* est inhaerens; adhaeret substantiae vel naturae; indiget subiecto sub ipso *esse* stante; diversum proinde est *esse* et *id quod est.*"[14] Although these are just a few examples of the traditional philosophical speculation

---

11   "Diversum est esse et id quod est; ipsum enim esse nondum est, at vero quod est accepta essendi forma est atque consistit" (*Quomodo substantiae in eo quod sint bonae sint cum non sint substantialia bona* [=*De hebdomadibus*], 2nd thesis: PL 64,1311; and also in *Boethius: The Theological Tractates and the Consolation of Philosophy*, ed. by H. F. Stewart and E. K. Rand, 7th rpt. [London & Cambridge, Mass.: William Heinemann & Harvard University Press, 1968], p. 40). An erudite revision of the interpretations of Boethius's thesis is found in R. McInerny, *Boethius and Aquinas* (Washington, D. C.: The Catholic University of America Press, 1990), Part Three: "*De Hebdomadibus,*" pp. 161–231.

12   *In VIII De div. nomin.*, lect. 1, n. 751.

13   *Quodlib. I* q. 9, in *Quodlibeta Magistri Henrici Goethals a Gandavo Doctoris Solemnis* (Paris, 1518), reprint (Louvain, 1961), fol. 7v, quoted by J. F. Wippel, *The Metaphysical Thought of Godfrey of Fontaines: A Study in Late Thirteenth-Century Philosophy* (Washington, D. C.: The Catholic University of America Press, 1981), pp. 83–84, note 120.

14   N. del Prado, O.P., *De veritate fundamentali philosophiae christianae*

on the distinction of being and the act of being, nevertheless they are sufficient to show that Heidegger's complaint about its supposed neglect in the history of philosophy is unfounded.

Heidegger's erroneous appraisal of the historic record on the difference of being and *Sein* led him to present himself as the first philosopher to bring it to light, and consequently to put an end to its concealment throughout the long tradition of Western metaphysics. But finally Heidegger said that the concealment of the difference between *Sein* and being was an intrinsic failing of the ontotheological constitution of first philosophy. According to his own definition, metaphysics is thought about being wherein God "entered" as an essential requirement of philosophy.[15] Now then, God "entered" into ontotheology insofar as he is thought, but thought, Heidegger said in following Hegel's teachings, "is the subject of logic."[16] However, the ill-defined modern usage of the word *thought* led him to neglect the differences between the multifarious acts involved indiscriminately in the signification of this word. So, in assigning such a subject to logic, Heidegger not only rejected the epistemic specification of this science, but he also identified it as a *metaphysica generalissima*, transformed virtually into an omniscience, in a sense that fully agrees with the character of the *Wissenschaft der Logik* of Hegel's system.

It is well to remember that most Hegelian thinkers tried to bring the chief principles of Hegel's logic back to theoretical grounds presumably extracted from Aristotle's philosophy, but this attempt always ended in failure. As one casts a glance at the Stagirite's speculation, its absolute incompatibility with the German author's idealist system is immediately apparent. That is why, not unlike Heidegger's Hegelian hermeneutics,

---

(Friburgi Helvetiorum: Typis Consociationis Sancti Pauli, 1911), p. 28, and *passim*.

15   Cf. "Die onto-theo-logische Verfassung der Metaphysik," in *Identität und Differenz*, pp. 52–53.

16   *Ibid.*, p. 54. Cf. *Was heißt Denken?* p. 145.

Herbert Marcuse announced in untenable terms this supposed Aristotelian basis of Hegel's pseudo-logic: "Hegel's
Logic expounds the structure of being-as-such, that is, the
most general forms of being. The philosophical tradition since
Aristotle designated as categories the concepts that embrace
these most general forms: substance, affirmation, negation,
limitation; quantity, quality; unity, plurality, and so on.
Hegel's *Logic* is an ontology insofar as it deals with such categories. But his *Logic* also deals with the general forms of
thought, with the notion, the judgment, and of syllogism, and
is in this respect 'formal logic.'"[17] Marcuse's interpretation,
which involves a glaring misunderstanding of Aristotelian
logic, indeed conforms to the character of Hegelian *Logic*, just
as Heidegger understood it almost contemporaneously.[18]

Against Hegel and Heidegger, it is necessary to affirm
that logic is not the science of thought *ut sic*. Indeed, logic is
not the science of thought because it is not a general discipline
of knowledge or a gnoseology, but "the speculative science
and art of the being of reason of second intention, that is, of
the relations of reason between objective concepts."[19] No
doubt, the vague use of the word *thought* by modern philosophers and by Heidegger himself prevents a precise definition
of this act of knowledge so that its signification could be
exempt from confusion. By contrast, in the height of medieval
Scholasticism, once the semantic variability of the ordinary

17   H. Marcuse, *Reason and Revolution: Hegel and the Rise of Social Theory*,
     2nd ed., 3rd rpt. (London: Routledge & Keegan Paul, 1969), pp. 62–63.

18   On the nature of logic in Aristotelian philosophy, see F. A.
     Trendelenburg, *Elementa logices Aristoteleae*, 9th ed. (Berlin: Weber,
     1892); H. Maier, *Die Syllogistik des Aristoteles*, 2nd ed. (Leipzig: Köhler,
     1936); F. Solmsen, *Die Entwicklung der aristotelischen Logik und Rhetorik*
     (Berlin: Weidmann, 1929); P. Gohlke, *Die Entstehung der aristotelischen
     Logik* (Berlin: Junker & Dünnhaupt, 1936); and E. Weil, "La place de la
     logique dans la pensée aristotélicienne," *Revue de Métaphysique et de
     Morale* 56 (1951) 283–315.

19   J. A. Casaubon, "Lógica y 'lógicas'": *Estudios Teológicos y Filosóficos* 1
     (1957) 166. Cf. 68–86, 140–72 and 230–48.

use of the word *cogitatio* had been noticed, St. Thomas Aquinas was particularly careful in observing that it means an actual intellective consideration, sometimes the act of the *vis cogitativa*, and also an investigation ordered to understanding.[20]

But the modern *Denken* extolled by Heidegger is not just any kind of thought either; it is the very *Denken* sublimated to an unheard-of degree in Hegel's *Science of logic*. This Hegelian *Denken* arose from a λόγος which would monopolize the entire truth of *Sein* through the institution of logic as an all-inclusive science of everything that is since, after all, it is claimed to be the prototypical science, the quintessential science of *Sein*, and, in the last analysis, the pure thought that would allegedly develop in history its own divinity. Consider this impressive statement of Hegel: "Logic is consequently to be understood as the System of Pure Reason, as the Realm of Pure Thought. *This realm is the Truth as it is, without husk in and for itself.* One may therefore express it thus: this *shows forth God as he is in his eternal essence before the creation of Nature and of a Finite Spirit.*"[21] And this pantheistic *Denken* of Hegel's system, according to his own declaration, is the very same thought that stimulated Heidegger to think about *Sein* as a pure *Sein.*[22] Therefore, it is not surprising that Heidegger, in following a Hegel who enormously enlarged the scope of the

20   "Cogitatio tripliciter sumi potest. Uno modo, communiter pro qualibet actuali consideratione intellectus. . . . Alio modo dicitur cogitare magis proprie consideratio intellectus quae est cum quadam inquisitione, antequam perveniatur ad perfectionem intellectus per certitudinem visionis. . . . Tertio modo, pro actu virtutis cogitativae" (*Summ. theol.* II-II q. 2 a. 1 resp.). Cf. *In III Sent.* d. 23 q. 2 a. 1 qla. 1a resp.; and *De verit.* q. 14 a. 1 resp.

21   G. W. F. Hegel, *Wissenchaft der Logik*, ed. by G. Lasson, 2nd ed. (Leipzig: Felix Meiner, 1948), vol. I, p. 31; translated by W. H. Johnston & L. G. Struthers: *Hegel's Science of Logic*, 4th rpt. (London & New York: George Allen & Unwin, & Humanities Press, 1966), vol. I, p. 60.

22   Cf. "Die onto-theo-logische Verfassung der Metaphysik," in *Identität und Differenz*, p. 41.

modern *cogito*, had identified *Sein* with the thought that would reveal it. This clause of Heidegger's synthesizes explicitly his personal feeling on the matter: "*Sein* reveals itself as thought."[23]

Deep in the confusion wherein these untenable positions about logic, metaphysics, and human thought reign supreme, Heidegger portrayed the science of common being – considered as equivalent to ontotheology – with features that are very far from their true nature. So these statements are false: "Metaphysics thinks about being as such, i.e., in general. Metaphysics thinks about being as such, i.e., as a whole. Metaphysics thinks about the *Sein* of being in regards to both the unity that delves deeply into that which is most general of everything, i.e., into that which has always the same value, and also the unity that is the foundation of everything, i.e., of that which is the highest of everything."[24] The falsehood of these propositions, which removes the roots of the Heideggerian argument about the ontotheological constitution of metaphysics – an argument taken from Kant's transcendental critique of knowledge –, can be proved by the following:

1) Metaphysics *does not think*, but the metaphysician *knows* in a scientific way, just as every man devoted to epistemic intellection does – apodictically – in order to deduce universal and necessary conclusions on the subject of his speculation. On the other hand, as a mere thought, metaphysics turns up stripped of every scientific specification, so that it is impossible to conceive it as the knowledge of which it properly consists, that is, a discipline that belongs to theoretical or speculative philosophy.

2) Being as such is not being in general, for the very term *ens generalissimum* – which underlies Heidegger's conception of *ens quatenus ens* as something equal to *Seiende im*

---

23 *Ibid.*, p. 54.

24 *Ibid.*, p. 55. My translation.

Allgemeinen – is damaged by a capital failure about which Aristotle had already warned with clairvoyance, that is, by no means is being predicated as a genus.[25] Insofar as a discourse on being in general is assigned to metaphysics, an insoluble hindrance for the determination of its proper subject is introduced. If being is not predicated as a genus, first philosophy cannot be ordered to the investigation of a subject that lacks the predicamental determinations that Heidegger has erroneously attributed to it.

3) Metaphysics *does not think* about being as a whole (*im Ganzen*), for the most universal predication of the *ratio entis* does not consist of an intellective reference to the sum of all the beings, although its definition does not exclude anything that is. So, the mention of all beings together is insignificant from a theoretical point of view because the notion of being is by no means either perfected or affected according to the amount of beings of which it is predicated.

4) Metaphysics *does not think* about the *Sein* of being in a supposed unity that would delve deeply into that which is

---

25 Cf. *Metaphys.* Bk. III, ch. 3: 998 b 22. Cf. Bk. VIII, ch. 6: 1045 b 5–7. Some texts of St. Thomas Aquinas enlighten and complement this Aristotelian thesis on the unpredicability of being as a genus; e.g.: "Sed in hoc decipiebantur [Parmenides et alii], quia utebantur ente quasi una ratione et una natura sicut est natura alicuius generis; hoc enim est impossibile. Ens enim non est genus, sed multipliciter dicitur de diversis. . . . Non enim habet unam naturam sicut unum genus vel una species" (*In I Metaphys.*, lect. 9, n. 139). "Nulla autem differentia potest accipi de qua non praedicetur ens et unum, quia quaelibet differentia cuiuslibet generis est ens et est una, alioquin non posset constituere unam aliquam speciem entis. Ergo impossibile est quod unum et ens sint genera" (*In III Metaphys.*, lect. 8, n. 433). "Nihil autem potest esse extra essentiam entis, quod per additionem ad ens aliquam speciem entis constituat: nam quod est extra ens, nihil est, et differentia esse non potest. . . . Ens, genus esse non potest" (*In V Metaphys.*, lect. 9, n. 889). "Nulla autem posset differentia sumi, de cuius intellectu non esset unum et ens. Unde unum et ens non possunt habere aliquas differentias. Et ita non possunt esse genera, cum omne genus habeat differentias" (*In XI Metaphys.*, lect. 1, n. 2169).

most general because, on the one hand, as was said before, being has no generic unity, and on the other hand, it has no unity capable of delving deeply into a generality absent from its predication. For the same reason, one does not find in being a unity that is the foundation of everything from which its concept is predicated because the supra-predicamental unity of that which is is not based on something immanent to the totality of all beings, since in this case being would also be reduced to a genus. Moreover, this Heideggerian clause also implies two additional difficulties: first, claiming a foundation for being without having previously demonstrated that it is something necessarily founded as such, or something that necessarily needs a foundation; and, secondly, the very claim for a foundation ends up proposing a regression *ad infinitum*, for a foundation of that which is must also be something that is, from which it follows that it must be a being that, in turn, would require a previous foundation and this another foundation and so on indefinitely, unless, instead of a foundation, the true claim points to an uncaused cause. But Heidegger's phenomenological ontology does not take into account this uncaused cause because he repeatedly rejected every theorization on the principle of causality.

Heidegger attempted to stipulate the ontotheological character of metaphysics under the influence of the theory of the *ens generalissimus* popularized by seventeenth- and eighteenth-century Catholic and Protestant Scholasticism and by the agnostic condemnation of first philosophy in Kant's works. Furthermore, he accepted Hegel's pantheistic portrait of the λόγος, which allegedly contains a satisfactory explanation of the logical character of an ontotheology destined to think being as such. The logic of λόγος is a thought about being founded on *Sein*, i.e., on a foundation that would be the very λόγος itself. So, the intrinsic logic of metaphysics is said to consist of a thought that always delves deeply into being as such and is also the foundation of every being as something included in the sum of all beings by virtue of the λόγος itself, or, what is the same, by virtue of the *Sein* as foundation.[26]

In this Heideggerian schema of the thought about *Sein*, both thought and *Sein* are related to each other within the same circuit that unifies the immanence of both the thinking λόγος and the *Sein* thought logically, which is the modernized Hegelian version of Parmenides' radical univocist monism later accepted by Heidegger, that is, to be and to understand are argued to be one and the same.[27] This Eleatic monism is found at the basis of all the philosophical theories that affirm the univocal predication of being as a genus. But if Hegel's thought is one of the most extreme modern expressions of that univocism, Heidegger not only did not raise any objection to the grave theoretical consequences arising from monist ontology, but, on the contrary, he echoed it by agreeably admitting the Hegelian identification of *Denken* and *Sein*, in which he found a profitable Parmenidean vindication of these acts. Heidegger made subsequent use of this vindication to discredit the presumed 'logicization' of metaphysics, the theorems of which would keep *Sein* unthought and forgotten, as he claimed has happened throughout the philosophical tradition starting with Plato and Aristotle.

Consequently, according to Heidegger, ontotheology is a logic of being – in the Hegelian sense – into which God "enters" as the most elevated thing and also as the foundation of all the beings unified by the *Sein* consubstantial to thought. But Heidegger asserts something else that determines to the utmost degree the signification granted to ontotheology, i.e., God "enters" into metaphysics as the most elevated being, as the founding being of every being, and therefore of Himself as well, because although He is the supreme entity, God is

---

26 Cf. "Die onto-theo-logische Verfassung der Metaphysik," in *Identität und Differenz*, p. 56. See also p. 67.

27 Cf. H. Diels, *Die Fragmente der Vorsokratiker*, 28 B 3, vol. II, p. 231, quoted *supra*, p. 2, note 1.

also a being, so that, according to its metaphysical conception, the divine being "enters" into first philosophy as a *causa sui*.[28] The Heideggerian explanation of God as *causa sui* carries along all the contradictions involved in this familiar and unfortunate formula, but the German philosopher adopted it in accordance with the variants proposed in the Modern Age by Descartes, Spinoza, and Hegel. Even more, when Heidegger wanted to justify it, he fell into one contradiction after another, for one cannot assert that something, whatever it is, is its own cause without violating explicitly the principle of non-contradiction. To verify this we ought to take into account that Heidegger affirmed that *Sein* founds being insofar as the former is the foundation of the later, but he said contradictorily that being founds *Sein* by causing it, that is, insofar as the supreme being of metaphysics is the height of *Sein* itself.[29] The contradiction is evident, for if *Sein* is the foundation of being, one cannot understand how the latter may be the cause of the former. Perhaps Heidegger could have replied that the being that causes *Sein* is not just any being, but the supreme being, or the being to which *Sein* as foundation belongs originally and paradigmatically, but this counterargument does not dissipate the aforementioned contradiction; instead, it increases it. Indeed, if the supreme being is an effect of any cause, as *causa sui*, its *Sein* would be neither paradigmatic nor original, but secondary and derived – therefore, it would not be the supreme being –, for every effect always follows a cause, and even this is inadmissible, for, in such a case, the supreme being would precede and follow itself at the same time. It would precede itself as its own cause

---

28   Cf. "Die onto-theo-logische Verfassung der Metaphysik," in *Identität und Differenz*, p. 57.

29   Cf. *ibid.*, pp. 66–68. Cornelio Fabro pointed out that this flagrant denial of the principle of causality refers also to the Heideggerian exegesis of Parmenidian-Hegelian univocism conceived as a reciprocity. Cf. C. Fabro, C.P.S., *Introduzione all'ateismo moderno*, 2nd ed. (Roma: Editrice Studium, 1969), vol. II, p. 960.

since every cause precedes its effect, and, moreover, it would follow itself insofar as it is an effect of its own causality, due to the fact that every effect follows its causes. But nothing can precede or follow itself, as in many places St. Thomas Aquinas irrefutably proved.[30] Imbued with the visceral immanentism of modern thought, Heidegger did not realize that the *causa sui* formula implies the most flagrant denial of the principle of causality known throughout the history of philosophy.

Heidegger's God as *causa sui* is not the *ipsum esse subsistens*, the uncaused cause of metaphysics. It is the pseudo-divinity of modern immanentism, which started with Descartes's *cogito*, and wound up in the ontologies of Spinoza, Hegel, and Schleiermacher as something identified with the world it would not transcend. This *causa sui*-God is the deity of the ontotheological caricaturization of the science of being as such, but it is not at all the pure act speculated within the theorems of first philosophy.

According to this Heideggerian sketch, ontotheology appears as a thought concerned with a transcendental introspection on itself insofar as it is something immanent to the knowing subject's consciousness. It claims to include a

---

30 "Secundum enim idem genus causae aliquid esse causam et causatum est impossibile" (*In V Metaphys.*, lect. 2, n. 774). "Idem non est causa sui ipsius" (*De verit.* q. 10 a. 13 ad 3um; *Summ. theol.* I q. 19 a. 5 resp., I-II q. 78 a. 1 ad 3um). ". . . Cum nihil sit causa sui ipsius" (*De potent.* q. 7 a. 8 resp.). "Nihil est principium vel causa sui ipsius" (*De malo* q. 13 a. 1 sed contra 3). "Nihil est causa sui ipsius; esset enim prius seipso, quod est impossibile" (*Summ. c. Gent.* I 18). "Nihil autem potest esse sibi causa essendi" (*Ibid.*, I 47). "Nihil enim sui ipsius causa est" (*Ibid.*, I 49). "Nec tamen invenitur, nec est possibile, quod aliquid sit causa efficiens sui ipsius; quia sic esset prius seipso" (*Summ. theol.* I q. 2 a. 3 resp.). "[Efficientes et materiales] causae in omnibus distinguuntur ab his quorum sunt causae: nihil enim est sua materia, neque aliquid est suum principium activum" (*Ibid.*, I q. 39 a. 2 ad 5um). Cf. N. del Prado, O.P., *De veritate fundamentali philosophiae christianae*, p. 88, note 2; and M. E. Sacchi, *El yo y la metafísica: La metamorfosis inmanentista del significado de la filosofía primera* (Buenos Aires: Basileia, 1997), p. 117, note 2.

comprehension of *Sein* as the foundation of being and to cul-
minate as a theology insofar as it theorizes about God as a
causa sui and supreme being. According to Heidegger, the
ontotheological constitution of metaphysics is something of
this sort. But of what metaphysics? Of the science of being as
such, the first philosophy that allegedly failed because of its
ontotheological sterility to furnish us with a thought on *Sein*
as pure *Sein*, for *Sein* is allegedly not a being, nor a logos, nor
anything divine, for even God is said to be just an entity of
metaphysics. Thus, it was not sheer coincidence that
Heidegger glimpsed that thought, in order to grasp the
"divine God," ought to attempt thinking without God, to
relinquish the God speculated by metaphysics, and, as if that
were not enough, to accustom one to believe that the extra-
metaphysical thought about God could be exercised with a
freedom that the ontotheological constitution of the science of
common being does not seem to be willing to grant to any
metaphysician.[31] Therefore, it is clear that the Heideggerian
thought about *Sein* discards the possibility of a metaphysical
knowledge of the true God, of the "divine God." In other
words, it is equivalent to saying that the deity speculated on
by philosophers is an idol of reason, or a fictitious deity. So,
the pure act or the uncaused cause of the science of being as
such is argued to be neither the very subsistent act of being
nor the first principle of all the things that are.

It is clear that Heidegger's thought about *Sein* does not
aim to be a philosophical theology, for he considered it to be
neither the science of a God that philosophy had invented in
defiance of the deity of religion nor the science of the act of
being that subsists as something identical with the essence of
the pure act. Heidegger's ups and downs with regard to this
matter have been incessant. He never asked whether there is
a God, what is his nature, or of what does his relationship
with the world and with man consist. He was repeatedly told

---

31   Cf. "Die onto-theo-logische Verfassung der Metaphysik," in *Identität
     und Differenz*, p. 71.

that his thought about *Sein* seems to lead to an atheistic position, but his response was resolutely negative and said that his thought did not involve any kind of atheism. But when he was asked to clarify his attitude with respect to the aporiae concerning the fundamental philosophical questions about God – *an est* and *quid est* –, he invariably sought shelter in escapism and in silence. For a long time many philosophers of different theoretical trends invited him to speak on the matter, but Heidegger did not accept these invitations. We do not even know if he held any personal conviction about this question. In spite of everything, it is evident that his evasions served to link him in a way, as strange as it is coherent, with the aim that dominates his thought about *Sein*, i.e., systematically professing agnosticism, but at the same time refusing to own up to being an agnostic himself. Hence Heidegger's escapism and silence with regard to the question of God raised every sort of conjecture from those who strove to interpret his thought about *Sein*, so that one can surmise, although without certitude, that the need to deal with such a question caused him some disturbance. At least, that is what one is likely to think in light of the subterfuges to which he permanently resorted in order to avoid its corresponding solution or, at least, to avoid trying to solve it.

Nevertheless, there is a suggestive detail in Heidegger's thought about *Sein* which seems to be closely bound to his escapism and silence in relation to the philosophical question on God: whereas he did not answer the aforementioned philosophical question, from the Second World War on a series of remarkable references to some mythical entities contrived by Hölderlin's poetic hallucinations were introduced into Heidegger's works instead. It is necessary to emphasize that these references are remarkable because there is a significant datum which, as far as we know, does not usually draw the attention of the interpreters of Heideggerian thought about *Sein*, that is, that Heidegger spared no criticisms either to the metaphysical conception of the divine being or to the divinity affirmed by faith, but, as counterweight, he never uttered a condemnatory word about the demiurgic chimeras which Hölderlin, during his attacks of madness, imagined under the stimulus of a recalcitrant neo-paganism. This neo-paganism had an unquestionable influence in the birth and the consolidation of German Romantic thought and even in the development of Heideggerian *Seinsfrage* in the postwar period.[32] At a certain point in time Heidegger accepted Hölderlin's theosophic mythology and incorporated it into his own thought about *Sein* as if it were a conception of indisputable philosophical value. Thus came about the Heideggerian exegesis of the much renowned pantheistic *quaternitas* extracted from Hölderlin's poems: Earth, Sky, Gods, and Mortals. According to Heidegger, this quaternary constitutes an original unity which encompasses the four chimeras into something that cannot hide its character as a substantial community and moreover, as though it were just a small thing, that is devised as a substitute for the Trinity of Christian faith.[33] But Heidegger's reference to Hölderlin's quaternary is not a mere reminiscence of a poetic expression invoked only

---

32 Jakob Hommes published an illuminating study on the nature of contemporary existentialism in which, among other concerns, he deals with the influence of Hölderlin's neo-pagan mysticism on the shape of that movement. Cf. J. Hommes, "Das Anliegen der Existentialphilosophie": *Philosophisches Jahrbuch* 60 (1950) 175–99, reprinted in Id., *Dialektik und Politik: Vorträge und Aufsätze zur Philosophie in Geschichte und Gegenwart*, ed. by U. Hommes (Cologne: Verlag J. P. Bachem, 1968), pp. 113–44.

33 Cf. "Bauen, Wohnen, Denken," in *Vorträge und Aufsätze*, pp. 139–56. Fabro observed that the incorporation of Hölderlin's *quaternitas* into Heideggerian thought implied a clear welcome to gnostic pantheism. See C. Fabro, C.P.S., "Ontologia e metafisica nell'ultimo Heidegger," in Id., *Dall'essere all'esistente*, 2nd ed. (Brescia: Morcelliana, 1965), pp. 399–401. On Hölderlin's influence on the process of the loss of Christian faith in Romanticism, particularly in German idealism, see G. Waldmann, *Christliches Glauben und christliche Glaubenslosigkeit: Philosophische Untersuchungen zum Phänomen des christliches Glaubensvorgangs und zu seiner Bedeutung für die Situation der Gegenwart* (Tübingen: Max Niemeyer, 1968), pp. 201, 234, 245 and 322; and also

to infuse a touch of elegance into a discourse that aspires to be of a philosophical nature. In fact, Heidegger appropriated this *quaternitas*, which Hölderlin dreamed up in order to theologize about its mythical signification to such an extent that he used it with the aim – no less – of cracking the 'essence' of everything, or of that which he called *the thing*. It is thought-provoking indeed that into writings contemporary with the one just cited, Heidegger poured the results of a dense thinking at the core of which lie, precisely, the functions assigned by Hölderlin to "the Four." Moreover Heidegger added to these results something more amazing still, namely that such a *quaternitas* is not attributed to the poet's authorship, but it is always quoted as a belief that Heidegger assumed and professed in a most personal way, i.e., independently of the source from which he extracted it.[34]

The readers of this book are free to judge the scope of Heideggerian thought about *Sein* once metaphysics and, with it, the philosophical theology of natural reason are discarded. Our own opinion on this matter is not new, for it has been expressed by several philosophers that Heidegger's thought about *Sein* pointed toward an esoteric gnosis inspired by Hölderlin's neo-pagan mysticism. From this point of view, Heidegger cannot be exempted from having joined the general current of twentieth-century existentialism, which expressed an open revulsion against every metaphysical vision of the universe and also against the participation of the sacred in human nature, such as Christianity conceives it. Even in Germany some authors justly noted this inclination of Heidegger's thought about *Sein* throughout the most intense stage of his development. Jakob Hommes stood out in this sense, but his energetic refutation of existentialist atheism, which is concerned with Heidegger more than with anyone else, was disregarded and disdained by all his colleagues.

---

the statements of J. Hommes, *Dialektik und Politik*, pp. 126, 134–37, 140, 159 and 171.

34   Cf. "Das Ding," in *Vorträge und Aufsätze*, pp. 157–75.

Hommes's reaction, also subscribed to with no less energy by Bernhard Lakebrink and Walter Hoeres, among other philosophers, did not succeed because of the fascination that Heideggerian thought about *Sein* aroused in the academia of the postwar period.[35] That thought not only captivated the philosophical guild; it also influenced many powerful theologians, mainly in the school infelicitously called *Transcendental Thomism*, among whom Karl Rahner was the outstanding figure. That is why it is necessary to retrieve the critiques of Heideggerian thought about *Sein* which Hommes, Lakebrink, and Hoeres pointed out; not only in light of their intrinsic philosophical value, but also because they contain the most illuminating reasonings about both the gnostic background on which such a thought is based and its incompatibility with the Christian faith. Not by chance, Heidegger's opinions on *Sein*, once absorbed by many theological works of the second half of the twentieth century, plunged the thinking of experts in *sacra doctrina* into the most oppressive crisis to affect this science throughout the entire Modern Age.

---

35 Cf. J. Hommes, *Zwiespältiges Dasein: Die existentiale Ontologie von Hegel bis Heidegger* (Freiburg im Breisgau: Herder, 1953); Id., "Das Anliegen der Existentialphilosophie," quoted; Id., "Der Existentialismus – Ein neuer Glaube": *Philosophisches Jahrbuch* 61 (1951) 314–41, reprinted in Id., *Dialektik und Politik*, pp. 145–82; B. Lakebrink, *Klassische Metaphysik: Eine Auseinandersetzung mit der existentialen Anthropozentrik* (Freiburg im Breisgau: Rombach, 1967); Id., "Die thomistische Lehre vom Sein des Seienden im Gegensatz zu ihrer existenzialen und dialektische Umdeutung," in W. P. Eckert, O.P. (Ed.), *Thomas von Aquino: Interpretation und Rezeption. Studien und Texte* (Mainz: Matthias-Grünewald-Verlag, 1974), pp. 48–79; and W. Hoeres, *Kritik der transzendental-philosophischen Erkenntnistheorie*, quoted.

Chapter IV

An Illusory Extra-Metaphysical Thinking About Sein

Heidegger believed that metaphysics was disappointing with respect to thought about *Sein* because it was confined to speculation on being as such – now on being in general, now on the supreme being – and this caused it to neglect *Sein*. Hence *Sein* is supposedly concealed in being, but first philosophy was said not only to lack the necessary capacity to grasp its truth, but also exposed itself as a certain kind of thinking, characteristic of Western philosophy, whose ontotheological constitution compelled it to forget *Sein* by preventing its disclosure and that its truth might be made manifest.

What is important in Heidegger's thinking is that he thought about *Sein* with the aim of facing and overcoming the supposed failure of both the epistemic structure and the historical development of the science of being in common. It is one of the latest and most industrious attempts of modern thought to eliminate metaphysics once and for all and particularly its sapiential extension toward the understanding of the first principle of the universe, which everybody calls *God*. In fact, Heidegger developed his personal thought on *Sein* under a conviction easily perceptible in his writings that, for him, *Sein* is not the essence of God. Once persuaded that *Sein* is not the quiddity of the divine being, he characterized his thinking about it as something different from the philosophical theology on which the theoretic nature of metaphysics is based. That is why he sketched it as a thinking about something he has called *Sein*, which, insofar as incapable of being thought by thought itself as the act of the things that are, ought to be thought as something immanent to the only thing that is neither something divine, nor hides it, nor forgets it, because the only task of such thinking would consist of disclosing *Sein* by revealing its secret, i.e., as something inherent in a human thinking that thinks of thinking itself.

Since Heidegger never admitted that *Sein* is knowable by man through the understanding of the things that are, of which it is their first act, one can understand why in his lecture "The Ontotheological Constitution of Metaphysics" – partially outlined in the previous chapter – he supposed that the metaphysician speculates on *Sein* identified with a λόγος that would act as a foundation, and finally of a *causa sui*. But this process defeated Heidegger's expectation. No one should have unfounded hopes about the possibility of metaphysics adopting the features of a thought on *Sein* as long as it continues to be linked to its ontotheological constitution, for in that case it would always remain such as it is, i.e., the science of being as mere being, but not a thought about *Sein* as pure *Sein*, or something of which the extra-entitative epiphany could not be apprehended through the exercise of the first philosopher's understanding.

According to Heidegger, the truth of *Sein* reveals itself neither from an inspection of the things existing in this world nor through metaphysical theorization, which would insist in keeping it hidden with a pertinacity set into its own ontotheological structure. So where do we find the truth of *Sein*?

Heidegger gave different answers to this question, but on a certain occasion he uttered something that deserves to be carefully pondered, namely, that the essence of being reveals itself in history, or, which is the same, its own history reveals its essence.[1] This assertion, at least, includes ingredients as amazing as they are disconcerting:

1) From *Sein und Zeit* onwards, Heidegger constantly dealt with the *essence* of *Sein*. This indicates that *Sein* is something endowed with a nature or a quiddity, for every essence is the *quid* of something. Consequently, it is necessary to discover whether *Sein* is identical with that essence or, on the contrary, whether it is something really different from essence. But in both cases *Sein* must be the *Sein* of something, and it is clear that Heidegger understood that it is something of being, for a thing, insofar as it positively signifies the essence of that which is, is convertible with being because of the act of being that makes it to be. Now, of what would the essence of *Sein* consist? Heidegger never said, despite having mentioned it incessantly. In principle, this duality may be interpreted in a double sense: either he knew the essence of *Sein*, but he refused to state it, or he did not know it, but he assumed that *Sein* would have an essence. In either of these alternatives, Heideggerian thought shows itself as something absolutely segregated from philosophy. The reason is obvious, for any supposed human knowledge of the essence of the act of being, or of the very essence of this act, would imply a knowledge of the being that subsists by virtue of its own nature, that is, the *ipsum esse subsistens*, which everybody calls *God*, although man's intellect, *in statu viae*, cannot know in itself the intimacy of the divine essence by means of its own natural powers alone. If it were so – i.e., if Heidegger did not know the essence of *Sein* –, his allusions to it have no philosophical stature, for philosophy cannot consist of a non-

---

1 "The history of *Sein* reveals its essence" ("Überwindung der Metaphysik," in *Vorträge und Aufsätze*, 2nd ed. [Pfullingen: Günther Neske, 1967], vol. I, p. 63; author's translation).

knowledge. Therefore, his references to the essence of *Sein* do not belong to the range of philosophical knowledge. This is why the lack of an unambiguous statement on the true essence of *Sein* in Heidegger's works implies that it remains hidden in the shadows of a mystery that cannot be disclosed through the analytics of metaphysical knowledge. Moreover, this mystery is said to escape the scientific field of philosophy and can be known only by a thinking of another kind – of a non-philosophical, and therefore non-metaphysical kind –, which, once philosophical theology and the fitness of philosophy to think about it have been rejected, requires the recognition of its novelty and exclusiveness in order to make amends for the ingrained vice of ontotheological speculation that began in Plato's Academy and Aristotle's Lyceum.

2) It is important to note that, according to Heidegger, the essence of *Sein* would reveal itself in *history*. But is this possible? History is the temporary compass wherein events happen one after the other, whose subjects are the changeable things of our world, but the act of being itself is not any event, so that historical events are not the best witnesses of such an act. Consider this example as confirmation: the battle of Waterloo took place in history on June 18, 1815, and, as is well known, it marked the decline of Napoleon Bonaparte's military and political career; but what act of being might have been revealed through this event? Perhaps one could say that it revealed "the being of the battle of Waterloo," which sounds extravagant. Perhaps the act of being was not revealed on that occasion, but was revealed in others. From which one could infer that there are some events lacking the act of being, which is still more extravagant. Again, it is clear that the act of being is not an event. If I wish to know the act of being of a stone, of a insect, or of man, it will not be revealed to me even by all the events of which these entities are the subjects. So, the assertion that the essence of *Sein* reveals itself in history invites one to turn his attention in another direction, that is, toward the imperturbable silence of

Heidegger's thought with respect to man's need to know the act of being as the very act of the things that are because of it. His postulation of a revelation of *Sein* in history is the other side of the coin of his tenacious unwillingness to speculate on things in order to know the act of being that makes them to be. Nevertheless, even if he were exempt from the need to think about *Sein* independently of the knowledge of the things which it entifies, it is still necessary to point out to him that human science, mainly philosophy, is not a knowledge of things insofar as they are subsumed into the historicity of the events of which those things are the subjects, but insofar as they are abstracted from particular and temporal contingencies. If I seek to know both what a horse is and why it is, my aim is to find out what concerns both its essence and its act of being, leaving aside the *hic et nunc* of every individual horse and of every particular aspect of its entity that may hinder or distract from the end that scientific reasoning pursues. Consequently, the Heideggerian assertion that the essence of *Sein* reveals itself in history means above all, but nothing less, that it would be useless to attempt to know it in the intelligibility of things which *Sein* itself entifies or makes to be. Still, Heidegger did not clarify what historical event would have revealed the essence of *Sein*. Perhaps one could guess that its revelation is not assigned to a concrete historical event, but to history as such or in its entirety; however, if this were so, such a revelation would remain dependent on a universal cosmic temporal process or to an unstoppable development which has not yet finished revealing itself so that both the extent of the history unknown by man and the possible extent of history yet to come tell us nothing, or nearly nothing, about it. So one may ask whether Heidegger is aware of the extraordinary smallness of man's knowledge of history that can give us only impoverished data about a *Sein* that reveals itself only in the gloomy factualness of an *Ereignis*. On the other hand, what about the meta-historical act of being of whose essential intimacy we have no natural evidence? This question leads to another : what natural certitude do we have about a *Sein* that is revealed in history but remains hidden in an inscrutable mystery? Heidegger did not pay attention to these problems that human reason would not even raise in the epistemic field of philosophy.[2]

3) Let us emphasize the most important aspect of the Heideggerian formula that we are dealing with, namely, that the essence of *Sein* is *revealed* in history. Once we associate the two previously noted characteristics – the mention of the *essence* of *Sein* and of its revelation *in history* –, and we put it together with the meaning of something that *in history* reveals itself according to its own *essence*, we find all the more reason to be astonished. Indeed, Heidegger offered no explanation of the motives that drove him to make such a statement. In any case, since he did not clarify his assertion, it lacks scientific stature insofar as the rationality of human science requires such claims to be essentially demonstrative; not merely enunciated, much less simply declared. But this is not the greatest cause of the stupefaction provoked by Heidegger's opinion; that is found in the midst of a rhetoric full of metaphors destined to exhibit his convictions by exacerbating the darkness into which his deliberately enigmatic thought always dissolves. In short, Heidegger uttered words that no philosopher had ever uttered as such or *in quantum huiusmodi*, for the formula "The essence of *Sein* is revealed in history" can only be stated by means of the assent of faith to the truths that the Word of God revealed to mankind.

Heidegger accused metaphysics of being an ontotheology incapable of thinking *Sein* as a pure *Sein* because all its theorems allegedly resolve into the most general concept of being,

---

2   Bernhard Lakebrink rightly demonstrated the impossibility of reducing the act of being either to an *Ereignis* (event, happening, episode), or to another form of historicity. See B. Lakebrink, "Die thomistische Lehre vom Sein des Seienden im Gegensatz zu ihrer existenzialen und dialektischen Umdeutung," in W. P. Eckert, O.P. (Ed.), *Thomas von Aquino*, pp. 48–79.

into which God "enters" as the supreme entity and, ultimately, as a being that, insofar as incapable of avoiding its supposed nature of a *causa sui*, would also need a foundation, even though God Himself would obtain his foundation from the very intimacy of His own entity. But this "God of philosophy," supreme being and *causa sui*, is too much of a being to be admitted as the foundation par excellence; indeed, it would not be the "divine God." There are many records throughout history of a "God of philosophy" contrasted to the "divine God," but it only appeared in Heidegger's works after the first stage of his philosophical development, namely, once he removed himself from the Catholic Neoscholasticism in which he was educated towards a philosophy expressly distant from that Catholic and Neoscholastic atmosphere. But besides the withdrawal from Neoscholasticism, this abrupt switch shows that Heidegger's inspiration in Protestant sources which, in accordance with the theoretical turn of his thinking from *Sein und Zeit* onwards, makes one suspect that they heavily impacted its gestation. To take an obvious example, in the twentieth century the contrast between the "God of philosophy" and the "divine God" became common currency under the influence of Liberal Protestantism, although by thinkers who preferred to express it as the antithesis *God of philosophers – God of faith*, which unfortunately has also been accepted inadvisedly by many contemporary Catholic theologians.

Some scholars suggested that it is in the relations between Heidegger and his friend Rudolf Bultmann, the most enthusiastic representative of a Protestant theology aimed at a *demythologization* of Christianity, that one can find the key to the mishap with which we are concerned.[3] Among many

---

3 An early sign of a certain influence of Bultmann in Heidegger's thought is glimpsed in the context of the latter's lecture "Phänomenologie und Theologie" delivered in Tübingen in 1927 and in Marburg in 1928. Cf. "Phänomenologie und Theologie," in *Wegmarken*, pp. 45–77.

others, Karl Barth and Karl Jaspers criticized the dependence of Heidegger's thought on Bultmann's theology, but other authors downplay such a dependence and, in a certain way, are inclined to neutralize it or reduce it as much as possible, as John Macquarrie did.[4] Nevertheless, among the interpreters of Heideggerian thought, the opinions of Barth and Jaspers seem to be more successful than that of Macquarrie. In agreement with Barth's and Jaspers's hermeneutics, Cornelio Fabro states, "[Bultmann was] the theologian [whose theories] were explicitly supported in Heidegger's atheistically inclined existentialism, that is, of an intrinsically finite being that by no means admits any possibility of reason 'going' toward God Himself."[5]

No doubt, Heidegger accepted the disjunction *God of philosophers – God of faith* on Protestant agnostic terms. One can see this without great difficulty by noticing the direction of his personal choice with regard to the thought about *Sein*. The *God of philosophers* is claimed to be neither the very subsistent act of being of the science of being as such nor the *Sein* thought by extra-metaphysical thought. It is not the *God of faith* either, for the religious man allegedly does not pray to nor adore the first and supreme being, the first unmovable mover, the pure act, the first uncaused cause – the *causa sui*, according to Heidegger's words. Of course, this theory rejects the existence of any harmony between the two divinities.

4   "It is a distortion of the facts to suggest that Bultmann takes Heidegger's philosophy as his foundation, and then tries to build the Christian faith on to it. Rather is it the case that Heidegger's existential analytic becomes for Bultmann a hermeneutic tool. . . . Heidegger's existential analytic helps to provide concepts for understanding the structures of human existence, and so enables us to formulate our questions clearly" (J. Macquarrie, *The Scope of Demythologizing: Bultmann and His Critics*, 2nd ed. [New York: Harper & Row, 1960], p. 167.)

5   C. Fabro, C.P.S., *L'uomo e il rischio di Dio* (Roma: Editrice Studium, 1967], pp. 393–94 (Author's translation). Cf. Id., *Introduzione all'ateismo moderno*, t. II, p. 950, note 14, p. 970, and p. 1098, note 5. See also J. Kraft, *Von Husserl zu Heidegger*, p. 99, note 64.

Thus, first philosophy and religious faith, because they are ordered toward very different deities, are said to be absolutely foreign to one another. So, in Heidegger's view, due to the fact that no conclusion of metaphysics can reach the *God of faith*, this science cannot act as an *ancilla* of a theological knowledge that starts from faith itself. Moreover, it is pointless for faith and sacred theology to resort to the theorizations of first philosophy about a God that has nothing in common with the "divine God." It is evident that this Protestant rhythm of Heidegger's thought, whoever was his immediate inspiration, reiterates verbatim the mischievous fallacy of the *duplex veritas*, vastly expanded throughout the Modern Age, that Luther's nominalist occasionalism and the main trends of the Reformation promoted.

According to Heidegger, thought about *Sein* perceives in the God of the science of being another case, although an outstanding one, of something that does not differ from the *entitas* of metaphysics and, moreover, which needs a further foundation. The metaphysician, accordingly, cannot grasp the true thought about *Sein*. Must one then resort to religion to think about *Sein*, where the sovereignty of the "divine God" defeats the "God of philosophy"? Again, Heidegger said nothing about this concern nor do his writings suggest that he wished to propose such a way in order to think about *Sein*. However, having rejected these two ways – metaphysics and religion – a thought about *Sein* that looks for the essence of the foundation has no alternative but to inquire for it right there where it is evident. But where? Certainly not in the entities that conceal it and in which it remains forgotten. On the contrary, it must be grasped *in the history that reveals it*. In history itself, because Heidegger did not conceive *Sein* as the very act of the things that are, so that its manifestation is not reached through the knowledge of being, that which *Sein* entifies, but through its happening (*Ereignis*), which is always a temporary event, since events only happen in time, the measure of motion exercised by material things of the universe.

This confirms that, if the act of being were an *Ereignis*, and if every event is measured by time, the act of being itself would have to be exhausted temporarily or to succumb to the finiteness of this world – *in-der-Welt-sein*. That is why it is necessary to admit that Heideggerian thought about *Sein* is permeated with a colossal immanentism.

Still, the *Sein* that does not show itself in its entifying immanence to things that are but only in history also does not show itself in the same manner that everything within the reach of the sensitive and intellective powers of the human soul shows itself, i.e., in exhibiting a sensibility and an intelligibility that causally attract our internal and external senses and even our intellect to be joined to them through the acts of sensitive and intellectual knowledge. Thus, *Sein* does not show itself as something naturally knowable in the light of mediate and immediate evidences of its entifying power in the universal sphere of things that are – those very things that, in exercising it, faithfully attest that the act of being is the intrinsic active principle by which they are and are what they are –, that is, all those things whose apprehension makes our scientific understanding fruitful, philosophy included. Far from it, only in history, not in things, Heidegger says, *Sein reveals itself*. Therefore, in revealing itself, it manifests itself in a manner radically different from the manner in which the things in the domain of philosophy disclose themselves, and, consequently, in the domain of a metaphysics dominated by the ontotheological frenzy of traditional Western philosophy. But this historical revelation of *Sein* is neither the act of the "God of philosophy" nor of the "divine God." The revelation of *Sein* is due neither to the God spoken of by philosophers nor to the "divine God" – who is apparently different from the former – so who then reveals the essence of *Sein*?

Heidegger asserted that *Sein* is revealed in history, but without offering any philosophical justification of his assertion. Perhaps he did not realize the implications hidden in his proposal. Among them we note the following:

1) A revelation requires a revealed message, somebody who reveals it, and an addressee to whom it is revealed. Let us start with the message. Heidegger said that what is revealed is *Sein* itself, *Sein* as *Sein*, or rather, according to his own words, the *essence* of *Sein*. However, the revelation of the essence of *Sein* cannot consist of the mere utterance of the verb *sein*, but it must contain an explicit declaration about its quiddity; e.g., it ought to say "*Sein* is this or that other thing." Nevertheless, having held that *Sein* is revealed in history, Heidegger did not say anything else about the message that supposedly stipulates what *Sein* is. If he had any evidence of its revelation, he did not tell us what had been revealed about *Sein*, at least publicly, so that the content transmitted through this presumed revelation remains apparently enclosed in his own soul and subject to his free will to transmit it or not to other men. Consequently, Heidegger took for granted that *Sein* would show itself through a hermetic revelation.

2) We know of just one addressee of the revelation of *Sein* in history: Heidegger himself. Indeed, if *Sein* is revealed in history, why did no one else throughout history acknowledge receiving this message up to the moment when Heidegger himself announced its historical revelation? He thus reiterated the esoteric intrusion into human thought of a hermetic revelation similar to the famous Cartesian discovery of the *mirabilis Scientiae fundamenta* in the military cantonment of Ulm during the night of November 10, 1619. This prompts one to see in Heidegger's criticism of metaphysics, and even in the eulogy of his attitude on the part of his admirers, the sign of a position impregnated with esoterism, for the revelation of the essence of *Sein* in history seems to have been addressed to someone exceptionally enlightened and selected to receive and guard a truth that no mortal would have known before Heidegger himself, not even philosophers. It is profitable to remember the Cartesian precedent of Heidegger's attitude. Descartes's esoterism is implied in his celebrated declaration "Cum plenus forem Enthousiasmo, et

mirabilis Scientiae fundamenta reperirem etc." transcribed by
his biographer Baillet.[6] Jacques Maritain pointed out the esoteric background of Cartesian thought with precision, which
now deserves to be compared to the revelation of the essence
of *Sein* proposed by Heidegger: "But the most remarkable feature of the discovery of this admirable science is that it comes
from above, being given to Descartes in a dream in which 'the
human mind played no part.' Lest any one think the philosopher was that day *plenus musto*, and 'that he might have been
drinking that evening before retiring to bed' . . . he takes care
to note himself that he had had no wine to drink for three
months. The enthusiasm which animates him in his solitude
has a divine origin, the intoxication of that night of November
tenth, 1619, is a holy intoxication, it is within him like a
Pentecost of Reason. As this *scientia mirabilis* was a personal
revelation to the philosopher, we can more easily understand
why the Cartesian doctrine has retained in several important
points the marks of a kind of collusion between what is
human knowledge and what is revelation."[7] A similar esoterism derives logically and naturally from the Heideggerian
postulation of a historical revelation of the essence of *Sein*, for
if *Sein* is knowable by man through the natural evidence of
the things that it entifies, what sense would its revelation
have? Surely, if the very entities of worldly things did not
vouch for the act that makes them to be, the knowledge of the
act of being would require that someone reveal it to men, but
its revelation, if it had indeed happened in history, had
allegedly been unattended up to the present. Mankind,
according to Heidegger, had forgotten *Sein* as a consequence
of a supposed oppression caused by the ontotheological

---

6   Cf. A. Baillet, *La vie de Monsieur Des-Cartes* (Paris, 1691), reprint
    (Hildesheim: Georg Olms Verlag, 1972), vol. I, pp. 50–51.

7   J. Maritain, *Le songe de Descartes: Suivi de quelques essais* (Paris: Éditions
    R.-A. Corrêa, 1932), pp. 26–27, transl. by M. L. Andison: *The Dream of
    Descartes: Together with Some Other Essays* (New York: Philosophical
    Library, 1944), pp. 26–27.

alienation of metaphysics. Therefore, men did not know the revelation of the essence of *Sein* in history until one of them – once he reported its universal oblivion, and was in possession of the truth of its essence revealed and lodged in his spirit, as he was its predestined receiver – had assumed the mission of proclaiming the mystery of a *Sein* concealed in being and scorned by first philosophy, but from then on completely ready to be thought by thought itself. Finally, Heidegger named himself as the repository of the historical revelation of the essence of *Sein*, as the *urbi et orbi* preacher of its truth, and also as somebody called to disseminate it with the authority of a prophet.

3) Lastly, who reveals *Sein* in history? Revelation differs from the simple natural evidence insofar as the former is the communication of a message by someone who teaches it to others, whereas conversely the latter is perceived through our immediate contact with things that are naturally manifest. But although Heidegger did not say who had been the revealer of the essence of *Sein* in history, it is logical to assume that the essence of *Sein* can only be revealed by someone whose essence is not only not foreign, strange, or ignorant with respect to such an act, but, on the contrary, whose essence itself is the act of being, i.e., someone whose act of being is his very essence or whose essence identifies with the act of being that he himself is. Now, if we leave aside the subterfuges to which Heidegger customarily resorted to avoid this question, we must answer that only God is His own essence and that nobody else, but only He Himself, has revealed to men that He is He who is (cf. *Exodus*, 3:14). Therefore, the revelation of the essence of the act of being in history is the divine communication of God's intimate life by the very being by essence. But this is a subject matter whose consideration is reserved to the experts on *sacra doctrina* proper, not to philosophers as such or *in quantum huiusmodi*, so that Heidegger, as a philosopher, dealt with the revelation of *Sein* in history by smuggling it into a philosophical pseudo-problematics

lucubrated behind true philosophy's back. Of course, philosophy is absolutely unable to face the revealed mystery of the *ipsum esse subsistens'* divine essence with the only instrument within its reach, that is, human reason insofar as endowed with no more than its natural powers.[8] In wanting to speak philosophically about the revelation of the essence of *Sein* in history, Heidegger fell into a theologism whose origin can perhaps be found in his youthful Scholastic education, even though this implies an antagonistic relationship to the core of Christianity, which does not admit that philosophy has the least prerogative to deal with the act of being whose essence has been revealed in history because its scientific consideration is reserved to sacred theology exclusively.

The gnostic character of the esoteric revelation of *Sein* proposed by Heidegger may also be noticed in the light of its uselessness for enabling us to know what *Sein* is. In Heideggerian thought, as opposed to the Christian understanding of the historical revelation of *Sein* – the living and true God has revealed Himself as the only God, who is Father, Son, and Holy Spirit, one according to His nature and triune according to the Persons –, the supposed historical revelation of *Sein* declares nothing about its essence. It does not say if it is an act of a cosmic, or human, or divine kind; one or multifarious, wise or ignorant, good or bad; if it is eternal, beautiful, and provident; if it is the cause of the universe and the father of every man or something non-related to worldly things. In the last analysis, the revelation of the essence of *Sein* that Heidegger imagined is damaged by absurdity, for it is a revelation by which nothing has been revealed: we know

---

8   "Relinquitur ergo quod cognoscere ipsum esse subsistens" – St. Thomas Aquinas said –, "sit connaturale soli intellectui divino, et quod sit supra facultatem naturalem cuiuslibet intellectus creati: quia nulla creatura est suum esse, sed habet esse participatum. Non igitur potest intellectus creatus Deum per essentiam videre, nisi inquantum Deus per suam gratiam se intellectui creato coniungit, ut intelligibile ab ipso" (*Summ. theol.* I q. 12 a. 4 resp.). But this is a conclusion of sacred theology about which philosophy has nothing to say.

nothing about its author, we cannot understand why this author has conveyed to man a news bereft of any message, nor why it has been historically postponed, awaiting an addressee who would put it into circulation once the human aspiration of thinking about *Sein* on the lines of the science of being as such had been set aside. Ultimately, what did the cogitative Heideggerian program reveal to us about the essence of *Sein*? Nothing. The truths that Heidegger had expounded about *Sein*, few or many as they may be, do not differ at all from the truth of the act of being which can be known or is actually known by metaphysical knowledge.

Heidegger sought to surpass metaphysics through a thought about a *Sein* that, in his opinion, reveals itself in history by showing its own essence. This is an anti-philosophical theologism insofar as it is associated with an esoteric hermeticism ready to contend with metaphysics for speculation about *Sein*, or to replace it by a genuine gnosis. But the new Heideggerian gnosis not only rejects the philosophical theorization on *Sein* in our own knowledge of the things that participate in it, but with that purpose it also invokes a historical revelation of the essence of *Sein* in terms that fail to hide a noteworthy paganizing appropriation of that which the Christian concept of ἀποκάλυψις involves.

As a result of all that has been said, Heideggerian thought cannot conceal its gnostic and illusory character. Illusory, because the massive criticism of metaphysics developed by Heidegger from *Sein und Zeit* onwards never managed to show how man's mind can know *Sein* in a way that does not coincide with the knowledge of the first principles and causes of everything, that is, with the knowledge of which the science of being in common itself consists. Gnostic, because Heidegger attributed the human ability to know *Sein* to a thought that does not consist of the understanding of things that are – the very same things that, insofar as they are beings, are universally theorized by the epistemic analytics of metaphysical intellection –, but neither is it based on a knowledge that depends on a true revelation, i.e., on the explicit message of a revealing agent whose very essence is the act of being. Thus, according to Heidegger, *Sein* is neither apprehensible through the knowledge of things which it entifies, nor the revelation of the essence of that which *is* being proceeding from the very subsistent act of the being who revealed Himself as the living and true God.

A suggestive indication of Heidegger's gnosticism may be glimpsed at in the silence that he kept about the biblical and Christian notion of revelation whenever he dealt with the supposed historical revelation of the essence of *Sein* that came into his possession. Indeed, insofar as it is incompatible with supernatural revelation, such as Holy Scripture, the revelation of the essence of *Sein* mentioned by Heidegger is a neo-pagan retrogression to the apocalyptic fabulousness typical of ancient mythologies, and, in spite of the passing of the centuries, still surreptitiously underlying the folk traditions of nearly all European peoples that had once converted from barbarism to Christianity. In fact, it is not too difficult to retrieve the family tree of the Heideggerian apocalypse of *Sein* through the study of the history of that Germanic literature he exalted with a reverential unction that invites one to compare it to the fruits of a mystical experience.

Quite the contrary, Christianity conceives revelation in an absolutely different way, e.g., "'Revelation' has a double signification – passive and active – that must be preserved in every analogical application. *In a passive sense*, it means a new knowledge of an exogenous origin, that is, received, not 'invented' by the activity of a [thinking] subject. [So], I did not find in myself what is revealed, for I got it from outside. *In an active sense*, it is this very action as exercised on the mind from outside to instruct it. Therefore, it is an action that cannot come but from another intellect that knows a truth and makes it known."[9]

---

9   J.-H. Nicolas, O.P., *Dieu connu comme inconnu: Essai d'une critique de la*

This common description of revelation is the basis of its Christian notion, but it is not fulfilled in the Heideggerian capriciousness of the revelation of the essence of *Sein*, for the latter contains neither a transmissible message nor an identified agent who communicates it, although it would be destined to a single receiving subject – Heidegger himself. So, this supposed revelation confirms *a fortiori* the hermetic character of the esoteric gnosticism of which it consists, because a revelation without a revealer and, besides, deprived of a concrete message, simply reveals that somebody considers himself its repository. Nevertheless, strictly speaking, the author of this gnostic machinations of a historical revelation of *Sein*, even lacking a revealing agent, may be identified without any difficulty – Heidegger himself. Nevertheless, it implies that a determinate message is revealed through such a supposed revelation, i.e., Heideggerian thought about *Sein* itself.

---

connaissance théologique (Paris: Desclée De Brouwer, 1966), pp. 193–94 (Author's translation).

Chapter V

The Replacement of Metaphysics by an Ontologistic Gnosis

Persuaded of metaphysic's failure at inquiring into the truth of *Sein* which it supposedly would have forgotten,[1] Heidegger tried repeatedly to outline a thinking about Sein freed from the ontotheological content attributed to the science of being in common. Any return to metaphysical speculation would keep us prisoners of the demise in which the historical development of this discipline had ended. But the assertion of this demise does not arise from a formal philosophical examination; it is the manifestation of an affectivity offended by the dissatisfaction that the memory of the science of being as such caused in Heidegger's spirit. From a definite moment of his life onwards, he insisted on blaming metaphysics for both the crisis and the straying of our civilization, although he adopted this point of view on the basis of an impression of history and of human culture tinged with melancholy and never supported by the documentary data that could allow him to verify such raving. This impression is

---

1   Cf. "Überwindung der Metaphysik," in *Vorträge und Aufsätze*, 2nd ed., vol. I, p. 65.

combined with a feeling of displeasure at the sight of a panorama sketched through a skillful scenographic craft from a watchtower installed on a summit embracing history and the contingency of all the worldly events omni-comprehensively.

Like many modern thinkers, Heidegger does not seem to see how much of his own personal subjectivity and his naïve trust in his information about history have conditioned such impressions, which, as it may be seen, are quite far from consisting of a true philosophic stipulation of the things which epistemic reason can speculate about. But the weaknesses of these non-philosophical Heideggerian opinions about the deplorable consequences that Western metaphysical theorization stimulated met with success among his disciples and admirers, to such an extent that his thought still captivates a legion of proselytes who go nostalgically on pilgrimage to the Black Forest encouraged by the same illusion that once emboldened pagans to go to the temple at Delphi and to other places set aside for religious meditation with the aim of discovering the meaning of the existence of man in this earthly banishment.

With his eyes fixed on a time and a place that would reflect the fateful dominion of metaphysics on spirits in Western Europe in the twentieth century,[2] Heidegger fostered an overcoming of this science as a necessary step toward the modeling of a thought ordered to save *Sein* from the oblivion into which ontotheological speculation had plunged it. Allegedly the historical heritage of the metaphysical tradition accustomed us to prolong indefinitely the misfortune of living and thinking by exercising a thought that forgets to think about *Sein*, to exclude it from our inquiries, and to forget it in the darkness of a bottomless truth.[3]

According to Heidegger, metaphysics is guilty of introducing into civilization a fateful thought which is the prelude

---

2   Cf. *ibid.*, pp. 69–70.

3   Cf. *ibid.*, p. 76.

to a determinate mode of historical human existence that gives him a patent annoyance. Surely, faced with this matter, Heidegger had a good chance to deal with something he never approached fittingly, namely ethics. He never devoted any attention to the morality of human acts. That is why in his works, instead of any discussion of the requirements of moral philosophy, there are somber allusions to the disappointment that he felt at the observation of deeds and acts because of the very condemnation that they provoked in his spirit. In his thought, the place of ethics was taken by sullen ruminations aimed at expressing sorrowfully the exasperation that some behaviors and historical events caused to him, although without indicating the reasons for their supposed illicitness. This reconfirmation of the affective atmosphere that dominated the development of Heidegger's thinking is a valuable sign to assess one of the most determining features of his thought about *Sein* sketched as a substitute of metaphysics, for this thought has been outlined entirely within the framework of the strange Heideggerian vision of man's implantation in the world and in history.

Indeed, Heidegger's thought about *Sein* started simultaneously with a conviction sustained without subsequent change from the publication of *Sein und Zeit*, namely, that man has been thrown into the world, a condition Heidegger called *Geworfenheit*.[4] But the image of man has a gravity that deserves to be noted because it explains why human thought on *Sein*, as Heidegger described it, is not the philosophical speculation on the things which that act entifies, but a thought about a *Sein* thinkable by thought itself that leaves aside its inherence in the beings that participate in it.

The Heideggerian thought about *Sein* is the same thought that *Dasein*, the human existent, would exercise as a subject thrown into the world. So to be thrown into the world is man's factual condition, but a condition which is not defining,

---

4   See *Sein und Zeit*, § 38: "Das Verfallen und die Geworfenheit," pp. 175–80.

since *Dasein* has not been thrown therein to occupy a determinate place once and for all, as if it were a consummated and
irreversible fact. Man would be thrown constantly into the
world, with no intermittence, in such a way that being
thrown therein marks the very *Sein* of *Dasein* and the factualness of his existence.[5] But what allows one to say that the
human being is a thing thrown into the world? Who, what
cause, or what power would throw him into the world wherein he would obtain the existential factualness of being in the
world itself? Does *Dasein's* act of being become exhausted
and wasted away in his factual existence in a world into
which it has been thrown? What dignity would the rational
animal have if his entity were lowered to the level of a thing
thrown into the world? Is this thing thrown into the world the
true man of body and soul who stands out in the universe
above any other creature? Perhaps Heidegger took heed of
the fact that his proposal of a thought about *Sein* exercisable
by a thing as miserable as this, one allegedly thrown into the
world, must necessarily be an act proportioned to the entitative misery assigned to the human subject and, on the other
hand, that such a thought is something absolutely dispropor-
tionate to the epistemic and sapiential eminence of metaphysics, the *domina scientiarum* that he wished in vain to overcome.

Man is by no means a thing thrown into the world. On the
contrary, so excellent is his nature that only he himself is
capable of speculating on everything – on his own entity, and
even about the act of being that makes every being to be in act

---

5   Cf. *Sein und Zeit*, p. 179. Juan Ramón Sepich conjectured that the affirmation of *Dasein's* factualness dissents from another previous
Heideggerian one, i.e., that the *Sein* of a human existing being would
consist of 'to can be,' or of being its own possibility (*Ibid.*, p. 143). The
plain truth is that Sepich was not wrong because the lack of any philosophical rigor in Heidegger's thought led him to fall frequently into
incoherence and contradiction of this sort. Cf. J. R. Sepich, *La filosofía de
Ser y tiempo de M. Heidegger* (Buenos Aires: Editorial Nuestro Tiempo,
1954, p. 336).

thanks to the power of a unique entifying act: the act of being itself. If the human being had the imaginary condition of a thing thrown into the world, he would not devote himself to thinking about the act of being, but to despairing of the miserable condition of his own entity, that is, of an entity absurdly implanted in the universe to dissolve itself into the temporary and provisional factualness of its *Sein*, because *Sein*, according to Heidegger, can only be *in-der-Welt-sein*. Not in vain have some interpreters of his thought believed that his portrayal of man involves an explicit nihilistic position. But this Heideggerian view of man as thrown into the world derived from the influence of affective and therefore extraphilosophical factors, because one cannot affirm that man is thrown therein unless this affirmation be supported by a distortion both of the rational animal's essence and of the causes of his act of being and of his second acts. Nobody can say that the human being has the condition of someone thrown into the world without objecting in terms of the authentic concept of man and without discarding the science that demonstrates what his place in this world, and in the whole universe, is. Moreover, this affirmation is governed by a primordial affective urge because it emphasizes that man, as a thing thrown into the world, is substantially a subject destined to endure his historical existence as if it were a tragedy that Heidegger's existentialist determinism – a coherent extension of the Romantic groans of Hölderlin, Nietzsche, and Rilke – inserted universally and inescapably into the rational creature's very quiddity. The drama of this neo-pagan dramatization of a man thrown into the world and lost in history was the aesthetic ambit within which Heideggerian thought about *Sein* has been hatched and grown affectively with the express intention of replacing the metaphysics of the Western philosophical tradition.

But is it possible to go back to this presumed failure of metaphysics in its vain attempt to disclose the truth of a *Sein* which it is said to have forgotten by persistently speculating about being in common? It is useless to ask Heidegger for the answers to the countless questions that he himself posed in his writings. He answered all these questions by framing other questions and, when his thought seemed to approach some moderately enlightening answer to what had been asked, an avalanche of allusions camouflaged as an anthology of undecipherable allegories only increased the silence into which his lucubrations habitually end. Heidegger subtly cultivated a mysticism that ended up pervading his very personal expository style. Moreover, there are serious reasons to believe that it is this mysticism – not the philosophical propositions scattered through his works – that is most admired in Heidegger's thought by those who, instead of receiving and developing those propositions with the firmness of apodictic arguments, surrender to the allurement caused by the authority today's culture has granted him: *Magister dixit.*

The character of Heidegger's thought cannot be explained if one does not bear in mind his hostility toward metaphysics. Heidegger created a fiction in his own mind that he called metaphysics, one that at most involves fragmentarily and deficiently teaching of some thinkers who cannot avoid their responsibility for the modern deterioration of the meaning of authentic first philosophy. Even so, it must be said without the slightest hesitation that Heidegger ignored what metaphysics properly is. Ultimately, his sharp criticism of what he erroneously assumed the science of being as such to be was as inefficacious as harmless because that science emerged unscathed by a rival who mistook his enemy.

However, it cannot be denied that Heidegger's clash with a fictitious metaphysics has a positive side, for in this struggle he devised, slowly and with great trouble, a *sui generis* system of thought. In our opinion, three features stand out in the structure of the Heideggerian system of thought, two of which were just noted: firstly, the act of being would not be the act of the things that are; secondly, the thought about *Sein* is intended to be a thought about *Sein* as such, whose essence would reveal itself in history; and thirdly, *Sein* would be thinkable starting from a preconception which would inhere in the thinking subject's consciousness in advance of knowledge of any being. Let us analyze these three features.

Heidegger never admitted that *Sein* is the act of the things that are. Perhaps it will seem an exaggeration to say that, for him, *Sein* would be nothing *of* being, for sometimes Heidegger assigned it a certain function in the entitative structure of that which is. Thus, among the different meanings that *Sein* has in his writings, Heidegger often indicated that it is the "presence of the present."[6] Nevertheless, most of his allusions to *Sein* are covered with an exorbitant proliferation of metaphors bordering on unintelligibility. The following statements are illustrative: *Sein* would be the "most empty and the most common of everything," "the most comprehensible and the most hackneyed," "the most reliable and the most said," "the most forgotten and the most coactive," "the exuberant and unique," "the concealment and the origin," "the abyss and the silencing," "the interinserting memory and the liberation," and so on.[7] But, on the other hand, it is no less true that his incessant emphasis on the 'ontological difference' of *Sein* and being allows a glimpse into an irreducible strangeness between them.

The strangeness of being and *Sein* seems inescapable because of Heidegger's constant affirmation of the concealment of the latter in the former. *Sein* would be in some state of estrangement or separation in relation to being itself; if not, the concealment of *Sein* in that which is would obstruct the possibility of knowing it through the 'ontological difference' that distinguish them from each other, however man's mind

---

6   Cf. "Was heißt Denken?" in *Vorträge und Aufsätze*, vol. I, p. 135; "Platons Lehre von der Wahrheit," in *Wegmarken*, p. 223; "Der Satz der Identität," in *Identität und Differenz*, p. 24; *Was heißt Denken?* pp. 41–42. And *passim*.

7   Cf. *Grundbegriffe*, ed. by P. Jaeger (Frankfurt am Main: Vittorio Klostermann, 1981), in *Martin Heidegger: Gesamtausgabe*, vol. LI, p. 68.

grasps it. Therefore, due to the fact that Heidegger dealt incessantly with *Sein*, one must admit its intrinsic knowability, in spite of the obstacles arising from its bond with the being wherein it remains concealed.

Heidegger always alluded to *Sein* as something of being *das Sein des Seienden*, but what function does *Sein* have in being? His innumerable answers to the question did not clarified the query, for *Sein* is only the act of being as such, but Heidegger never even glimpsed it. Thus, if he never declared that being is the act of that which is, why is being? Why are the things that are? What is *Sein* in relation to the things caused by the only entifying act?

Metaphysics establishes that the solution to these questions, as could not be otherwise, depends directly on the enlightening power of the principle of causality applied to the demonstration of the real composition and distinction of the act of being and the essence of finite things existing in the world in which we live and philosophize. Therefore, these questions would remain unanswered if the principle of causality is not duly understood. But Heidegger seldom referred to the principle of causality; he did not understand the aforesaid composition and distinction beyond its reduction to the dyad *essentia-existentia* picked up from the decadence of mediaeval Scholasticism and its aftermath, and, ultimately, he remained silent about the most pristine evidence of the act of being apprehended by philosophical reason in analyzing the things that are the objects of its epistemic discourse, that is, that the act of being entifies everything as its own act, as the first act of being as such. That is why Fabro believed that Heidegger's use of the dyad *essentia-existentia* explains his endorsement of a distinction of another kind, i.e., the distinction of the *esse essentiae* and the *esse existentiae*. This attitude connected him with the nucleus of Henry of Ghent's and John Duns Scotus' ontologies, which played a capital role in the development of modern thought from Suárez onward.[8]

---

8   Cf. C. Fabro, C.P.S., "Ontologia e metafisica nell'ultimo Heidegger," in *Dall'essere all'esistente*, pp. 412–19.

Indeed, if the act of being were not the act of that thing conceived as a being, the latter would be independent of the only entifying cause. Its *raison d'être* would inhere just in its own entity, and every being, as such, would contain and exhaust the self-sufficiency to be and to be what it is – a being. At the same time, the act of being itself, provided that it is something of being, would not have any function to fulfill were it not known why it inheres in it, unless to become present innocuously to suffer an insipid concealment. But if one infers from our knowledge of the universe of all existing things that the reciprocal strangeness of *Sein* and being would give rise to such chaotic perspectives, then the metaphysical necessity of the intellective ascent to the speculation of the very subsistent act of being, at least to the degree that it is within the reach of philosophical analytics, reveals that Heidegger did not open a path suitable to understanding the act of being as something absolutely transcendent with regard to all the things that finitely participate in it.

According to Heidegger, *Sein* is not infinite so that it is not the divine principle of the universe either. In using another inscrutable expression, Heidegger said that *Sein*, on the contrary, would be 'the near,' or even better 'the neighbor' (*Nächste*), i.e., something close to us, but at all events it would be far short of an infinity that he never attributed to it.[9] Therefore, *Sein* would be neither the act of beings that finitely participate in it, nor even less the pure act of the nature of the being by its essence. So, *Sein* would become exhausted in the manner of something immanent in the finiteness of things existing in this temporary world, none of which has infinity as an attribute of its essence.

Not being the act of being, thinking about *Sein* would aim to think about itself as a pure *Sein*, or in its very essence. But it is also necessary to be forewarned with respect to the Heideggerian use of the word *essence* (*Wesen*). Heidegger inquired incessantly about essences. One cannot object to this

---

9   Cf. "Brief über den 'Humanismus'" in *Wegmarken*, p. 328.

questioning insofar as the essence of things involves the *quid* of all of them, that which we inquire about when we want to know what they consist of. But his questioning about essences reached unwonted bounds, for he was not aware of the dangers that threaten philosophical speculation when essential contents are attributed to some things which, strictly speaking, are finite acts devoid of any quiddity or, at least, really different from the natures of which they are composed, from the substances in which they inhere as adventitious accidents, or from the subjects that exercise them as second acts. So, Heidegger's denial of the real distinction between the act of being and the essence of finite things led him to discuss, for instance, the 'essence' of the act of knowledge,[10] the 'essence' of the act of seeming as the act of appearing,[11] the 'essence' of being helpless,[12] the 'essence' of sensation,[13] the 'essence' of transcendental reflection,[14] etc. Yet, in addition to it, Heidegger also spoke constantly about the 'essence' of *Sein*, which, once its divine nature is denied, seems to attribute an essential content to the act of being whose presence is immanent to this world.[15] Then, the denial of the real distinction between the act of being and the essence of finite things is implicit in Heideggerian thought about *Sein*, as had already happened with the Scholastic ontologies of Henry of Ghent, John Duns Scotus, Ockham, Suárez, and many authors who have subscribed to the most diverse theoretical positions throughout the history of philosophy.

10 Cf. *Kant und das Problem der Metaphysik*, 4th ed. (Frankfurt am Main: Vittorio Klostermann, 1973), p. 110.

11 Cf. *Einführung in die Metaphysik*, 3rd ed. (Tübingen: Max Niemeyer, 1966), p. 76.

12 Cf. "Wozu Dichter?" in *Holzwege*, p. 281.

13 Cf. *Die Frage nach dem Ding*, 2nd ed. (Tübingen: Max Niemeyer, 1975), p. 162.

14 Cf. *Schellings Abhandlung über das Wesen der menschlichen Freiheit (1809)*, ed. by H. Feick (Tübingen: Max Niemeyer, 1971), p. 231.

15 For instance, among many other texts, *Vom Wesen des Grundes*, 5th ed. (Frankfurt am Main: Vittorio Klostermann, 1965) p. 50, reprinted in *Wegmarken*, p. 169.

Heidegger's thought about *Sein*, more than anything else, pretends to be a thought about the essence of *Sein* as such. But how to think about the very essence of *Sein* or about itself as a pure *Sein*? If being would hide *Sein* to the point of casting it into oblivion, it would be absurd to seek to think about it as something immanent to that which is. At the same time, due to the fact that every existing thing is a being, there is nothing outside of being itself. Outside being there is only non-being, or nothingness, which is nothing, so that the act of being must necessarily be found in the entitative range of that which is, for it would be ridiculous to suppose that the non-existent range of nothingness could be the range of the act of being itself. That is why being is the only range wherein its own act of being is found and manifest. Consequently, against Heidegger's theory of the concealment of *Sein* in being, it must be said that, inversely, it is being itself, insofar as it is thanks to the act of being that makes it to be and to be a true being, that shows that what is universally called the *act of being* imposes the conception of being on what it actively causes to be. Thus, a being or a thing is entified by the first act that grants it the *ratio entis* in a definitive way.

In spite of Heidegger's opinions, being is not a jail in which the act of being would be concealed, forgotten, and prevented from manifesting itself. Inversely, it is the act of being itself that makes a being something that is and, because of its own entifying virtue, that moves us to understand it as a being which such an act entifies. This is the profound meaning of Saint Thomas Aquinas' argument that the very noun *being* is imposed from the act of being insofar as it is the first act of things that are. The Latin participle *ens* does not entail a mere grammatical derivation of the verb *sum* because we predicate the *ratio entis* of beings that *are* thanks to the act of being that makes them to be and be what they are.[16] Thus, contrary to what Heidegger believed, being is revealed luminously and inalterably in its own entity to be and to be what

---

16 "Esse enim rei quamvis sit aliud ab eius essentia, non tamen est

it is because of the act of being that makes it to be and to be a being. Moreover, this act allows us to understand being as something that is insofar as we understand the very act that entifies being itself by our intellective grasp of the objectivity of that which such an act entifies. That is why to think about *Sein* in its own essence or as a pure *Sein*, as Heidegger insisted, is a desire which no man who philosophizes in this world may fulfill because, on the one hand, the act of being of the things around him has no essence or quiddity – as Aquinas said, the act of being is just an act: *Esse autem actus est* – [17] and, on the other hand, it is really distinct from the nature of things that exist by participation, i.e., those very things that such an act itself makes to be by its entifying causality. Only the act of being causes everything that exists to be, since there is nothing beyond the act of being that has the power of making something to be, and to be what it may.

To think the act of being as a mere act of being is also meaningless, for it is impossible to understand it outside the only range wherein it is knowable, i.e., in the intelligibility of the being that is by such an act. In any way it may take place, for our apprehension of the act of being happens concomitantly with our understanding of that which is insofar as it is, or, even better, of being as such, which is the proper subject of metaphysics.

That is why Jean-Luc Marion's reaction against the metaphysical 'idolatry' of being as such, or of the *ens commune*, from which he exempts St. Thomas, is not found anywhere in Thomistic philosophy. Aquinas himself restored the absolute necessity for the metaphysical understanding of being to know the cause by which it is a being and even the uncaused cause of all the things that participate in the act of being; so

---

intelligendum quod sit aliquod superadditum ad modum accidentis, sed quasi constituitur per principia essentiae. Et ideo hoc nomen Ens quod imponitur ab ipso esse, significat idem cum nomine quod imponitur ab ipsa essentia." (*In IV Metaphys.*, lect. 2, n. 558).

17 *Summ. c. Gent.* I 38.

much so that, for Thomism, the lack of such an understanding would eliminate entirely all intellectual knowledge.
Hence the Thomistic sentence, *Illud enim quod primo acquiritur
ab intellectu est ens, et in quo non invenitur ratio entis non est
capabile ab intellectu.*[18] And also this other, even more famous:
*Illud autem quod primo intellectus concipit quasi notissimum, et in
quod conceptiones omnes resolvit, est ens.*[19] That idolatry does not
belong to the understanding of the metaphysician as such
because our science cannot forsake its own subject; instead, it
has been imagined by Marion himself with the aim of launch-
ing a new agnostic rejection of first philosophy in the name of
its supposed impotence to conclude something about God
through the exercise of human reason's natural powers. This
aim is proven by his pejorative mention of the *metaphysica* as
something equivalent to that ontotheology condemned both
by Kant and Heidegger and, therefore, unable to obtain a
knowledge of the act of being in the fullness of its extra-entitative purity.[20]

A thought about *Sein* as a pure *Sein*, or in its own essence,
is only within the reach of an intellect whose understanding
is its own essence and its essence the act of being itself. If one
does not pretend that human thinking is the *ipsum intelligere
subsistens*, one must bow before evidence that dissuades us
from postulating a thought about *Sein* as a pure *Sein*. The act
of being is the essence of God, whereas being by participation
is something *quasi habens esse* in the measure that it has the act
of being as an act really distinct from its substance and, moreover, received in a composed and finite way within the
restrictive limits of its nature. So, if we join both Heidegger's
desire for thinking about *Sein* in its own essence and his aforementioned assertion that *Sein* would reveal itself in history,
we will become aware of the fact that he has proposed a

---

18 *In De causis*, prop. 6a.

19 *De verit.* q. 1 a. 1 resp.

20 Cf. J.-L. Marion, "Saint Thomas d'Aquin et l'onto-théo-logie," *Revue
Thomiste* 95 (1995), 31–66.

thought about *Sein* which would consist only of a thinking about the very subsistent act of being divinely revealed in history, but an act whose transcendence he denied in relation to all worldly things, its condition as an uncaused cause of every being that is an effect, and its infinity in act. Consequently, the essence of *Sein* would not be the quiddity of God. It would be the nature of something set inexorably within the finiteness of this temporary world from which it would differ only in the nothingness of an inscrutable great beyond.

We cannot know Heidegger's personal intentions, but that which he described as the thought about *Sein* as such entails an inevitable slide into an atheistic immanentism, at least implicitly, even though he did not admit that atheism was present in his system.[21] But that does not clarify the underlying problem, for in denying that God is the being by essence or the very subsistent act of being, Heidegger took away the speculation about *Sein* and about God Himself from the compass of philosophy and of sacred theology by transforming it, as Fabro said, into a "theophany of pure experience," which only indulgently may be differentiated from a mysticism completely at variance with the scientific and sapiential spirit that encourages natural reason and even Christian faith.[22]

According to Heidegger, the thought about *Sein* hidden in being and forgotten by the tradition of Western metaphysics would not be knowable through the understanding of the things that are because of *Sein* itself, of these very things around us throughout our worldly pilgrimage. Then, if we want to think about *Sein* in its own essence, we would need to fix exactly where and when we may grasp that which reveals itself in history. Yet no statement of Heidegger seems to satisfy the interest of the readers of his works when they

---

21 Cf. "Brief über den 'Humanismus'" in *Wegmarken*, pp. 311–60.

22 Cf. C. Fabro, C.P.S., "Ontologia e metafisica nell'ultimo Heidegger," in *Dall'essere all'esistente*, p. 403. This text of Fabro dates back to more than twenty years before Heidegger's death.

try to determine exactly his opinion on the matter. So great is the variety of positions he adopted on this matter that no one can know for certain what is the definitive or at least the preferred one, if he truly held any firm position on the question.

Nevertheless, in *Sein und Zeit* Heidegger included a paragraph that deserves to be recalled for it contains a concise synthesis of the necessary result of a thought about *Sein* that does not understand it as the act of the things that are or as the act of being as such. Indeed, he included in this book the following: it is necessary that man somehow find himself in the possession of the meaning of *Sein*, or rather that a certain knowledge of *Sein* be available before its explicit apprehension, for man would have a "comprehension of *Sein*" that would move him to ask for it. This "comprehension of *Sein*" would cause the formation of a concept that would signify it. So, even ignoring what *Sein* is, we would possess a comprehension of the *is* without having a determinate notion of this *is*. We would know neither the basis on which we could apprehend *Sein* nor its proper sense, but this implies that its comprehension would be a *factum*, a given fact immediately evident and prior to all questioning of *Sein*.[23] This is one of the outstanding theories of the Heideggerian system. It asserts that man must possess a knowledge of *Sein* prior to the formation of any concept in his mind. We would then have a comprehension of *Sein* entirely prior to any other knowledge such that *Sein* would be known by man as a *primum cognitum*. The reader may easily recognize that this kind of theory lies at the heart of the ontologism popularized throughout the Modern Age and even today.

The ontologism of Heidegger's theory becomes evident as soon as one notices that the human mind cannot acquire any knowledge of the act of being that would consist of a comprehension prior to the exercise of this act by the things that are. Even more strenuously, contrary to Heidegger's wishes, it must be said that our intellect knows the act of being

23   Cf. *Sein und Zeit*, p. 5.

through the understanding of its common or adequate formal object – being as such – without understanding previously the *is*, because the human intellect is capable of grasping neither the exercise of such an act independently of the apprehension of the subject that exercises it as its proper act, nor much less before it exercises it.

This Heideggerian theory is plainly ontologistic, since it assigns to man's intellect the power to perceive the exercise of the act of being before the perception of that which exercises it. But this is impossible. In the same way that I do not see John's act of sleeping, but John, who is sleeping, I cannot understand, much less comprehend, an act really distinct from the subject with which it must necessarily be really composed in order to be exercised and understood by a finite knowing subject such as man is. It is so because the *primum cognitum* of our intellect is neither *Sein* nor the *is*, but an object set before man's intellective power through a double specification: on the one hand, as an apprehensive capacity of a human soul joined substantially to an organic body, its proper or proportionate formal object is the essence of sensible things abstracted from the individualizing material conditions. On the other hand, inasmuch as man's intellect is a power naturally ordered to knowing whatever is, which does not exclude anything, its common or adequate formal object is being as such and, consequently, this order indicates that the human mind is potentially infinite, even though it knows actually and habitually just a finite and limited number of objects. Hence the first object knowable by our intellect is being itself, but not its act of being, so that we cannot know either its exercise of the act of being nor its second acts unless we apprehend the subject itself in which they inhere as things really distinct from its essence.

Heidegger's affirmation of a human comprehension of *Sein* before any other knowledge repeats the favorite slogan of ontologism, and, moreover, it also seems to admit the core of transcendental idealism. Heidegger said that *Sein* would not be known as the act of the things of the external world, that its essence would be revealed in history, and that man would possess a comprehension of Sein prior to his intellective perception of any other thing. But all this would be possible only if Sein was something immanent to the thinking subject's consciousness as something consubstantial with his spirit. In short, according to Heidegger, Sein would be self-consciousness, for its apprehension prior to the knowledge of any other thing could only happen if it inheres in consciousness itself as a connatural affection and, moreover, only in the measure that consciousness, by virtue of such a prior immanence of Sein in its entity, is in a perpetual act as something acted on by Sein itself, with which ultimately consciousness must identify.

The Heideggerian description of the way in which man's thought would come into contact with Sein cannot hide its unmistakable pantheistic character. No one can deny the perfect coherence of that description with his previous affirmation of the essential finiteness of a Sein grafted onto history to become exhausted in the time of the in-der-Welt-sein. If the absolute preeminence of the act of being does not imply its essential divinity, the summum that Heidegger attributed to it could not go beyond the horizon of worldliness, even though the entity of the man divinized by modern thought is the range within which Sein would reach its height after denying that the act of being is the infinite substance of God. Heidegger stated ex professo this pantheistic identification of man and Sein,[24] but his opinion was refuted rightly by Bernhard Lakebrink with the severity called for by the fallacy involved in its enunciation.[25]

The pantheism entailed in a thought about Sein proposed in these terms is undeniable. If Sein were to-be-in-the-world, its

---

24 Cf. "Der Satz der Identität," in Identität und Differenz, pp. 33–34.

25 Cf. B. Lakebrink, "Die thomistische Lehre vom Sein des Seienden im Gegensatz zu ihrer existentialen und dialektische Umdeutung," in W. P. Eckert, O.P. (Ed.), Thomas von Aquino, p. 54.

summum would be something compressed into worldliness exclusively. If the essence of *Sein* were not the very substance of God, its reduction to something infra-divine would imply that it subsists by virtue of the very nature of the things that exercise it finitely. If *Sein* were not God's quiddity, its optimum perfection would belong to some being placed in a self-sufficient universe which would be without being an effect of any cause that transcends it. If the essence of *Sein* were not the pure act, there would not be any God either and, therefore, the divinity would be inevitably a worldly thing. Finally, if man could think about the essence of *Sein* by means of his own natural knowing powers, this would only be possible insofar as a supposed original unity of *Sein* and human thought itself reflected their mutual consubstantialness, that is, in the measure that his act of thinking would be the *ipsum intelligere subsistens*, or, to say it according to the most favored formula of modern immanentism, insofar as the act of being is self-consciousness.

Chapter VI

A Metaphysical Cataloguing of Heidegger's Thought about Sein

Heidegger's criticism did not harm metaphysics. Its true nature does not correspond to the ontotheological constitution that Heidegger assigned to it, having accepted the proposal contained in the *Critique of Pure Reason* and echoing Kant's agnostic schema of the transcendental character attributed to man's knowledge. First philosophy remains intact after Heidegger reviled it because it is not an epistemic knowledge that forgot to think about Sein allegedly concealed in being and consigned it to ostracism. That is why Heidegger's verdict about the science of being as such with a view to solving the so-called *problem of metaphysics*, cannot be justified. Contrary to his opinion, that problem does not exist, since it is not a genuine aporia, as has been shown in the previous chapters. But Heidegger did not limit his thought to a mere extension of the modern condemnation of metaphysics, for he chose not one but many different alternatives to replace it, all of them intended to promote a thought about Sein as a pure Sein or in its very trans-entitative essence.

The Heideggerian thought about *Sein* did not result from scientific speculation undertaken in accordance with the proper method of philosophical analytics. Inasmuch as the observance of this method would have required him to respect rigorously the logical and metaphysical process he tacitly discarded, Heidegger opted for structuring a thought about *Sein* detached from every commitment to the ontotheological constitution that, in following Kant, he assigned to first philosophy. The character of such a thought, however, is incompatible with philosophical knowledge. The Heideggerian thought about *Sein* is a meditation deliberately disconnected from the experience of sensitive beings because it assumes a comprehension of *Sein* itself that would be immanent to human consciousness before any grasp of the things of the outside world, the only term from which, on the contrary, our soul may receive the intentional resemblances of objects intellectually knowable by the rational animal.

Is an innate idea the prior comprehension of *Sein* suggested by Heidegger? In part, so it seems, because it does not originate from an abstractive process rooted in a prior sensitive knowledge. On the other hand, in one of his frequent theoretical waverings, Heidegger also asserted that *Sein*, the very same *Sein* which we would know in that way, would reveal itself in history. Nevertheless, the three central elements that one can find in his theory – the concealment of *Sein* in being, its comprehension prior to the knowledge of any existing thing, and its historical revelation – have not been gathered together in a unified view, not even in a sketch endowed with a certain homogeneity. They appear in his works as stages in a search in constant development, modified successively insofar as he was engaged in newer and newer considerations on a thought about *Sein* contrived *ad libitum*, i.e., independently of the noetical order of philosophical reasoning.

Sometimes this, and other factors too, made Heidegger appear to be the protagonist of an anarchic regression to a sort of barbarousness out of his contempt for logical rules and the commonly accepted meaning of philosophical terms, and because he involved himself in trivial considerations alien to the true scientific concerns. For instance, let us recall the trivial magnification in *Sein und Zeit* of gossip (*Gerede*), which *Dasein* speaks denoting that it would be "inherent in the essential structure" of its *Sein*, to such an extent that even in idle talk the human being remains informed of the evidence of *being-in-the-world*, that is, of understanding it so articulately and fittingly that he would be able to involve and comprise entirely worldly beings. The shallowness of this position is patent, for, according to it, a deaf and dumb man, someone who neither hears nor utters gossip, would be prevented from obtaining a knowledge both of *Sein* and of being.[1] Sometimes Heidegger went back to the subjectivist nominalism of the ancient pre-Socratic skeptics in denying the intrinsic consistency of the entity of concrete things, now natural, now artificial, by reducing it to the mere *hic et nunc* of its appearing to the knowing subject; so this chalk would be a concrete thing, Heidegger says in plainly idealistic fashion, just because here and now it presents itself to me. Accordingly, any chalk I do not perceive is not a concrete thing.[2] A little bit later Heidegger opined that Christianity bears the greatest responsibility in the historical process of dedivinization, but of a dedivinization which, instead of excluding religiousness, would imply contradictorily and absurdly a transformation of our relationship with the *gods* into a genuine personal religious experience.[3] It is worth emphasizing the neopagan character of this incredible declaration. Further on, in regretting with his habitual melancholy the dehumanization arising from some imprudent uses of engineering, mistakenly identified *in genere* with technology as such, we see Heidegger engaged in a frothy discussion about the difference, which he reckoned as something very important, between a lever in the hands of an artisan and the levers of modern machines mechanically operated by factory workers. The comparison of these two kinds of lever led him

---

1   Cf. *Sein und Zeit*, p. 169.

2   Cf. *Die Frage nach dem Ding*, p. 21.

3   Cf. "Die Zeit des Weltbildes," in *Holzwege*, p. 70.

to ask "What about the lever?"[4] Now then, can it be sensibly affirmed that this question contains a genuine philosophical aporia? The Heideggerian literature abounds in this style of thought based on extra-scientific rambling and indeed devoid of philosophical stature.

Are those who see in Heidegger's thought something similar to a return to barbarousness unjust? No philosopher has the necessary authority to answer this question with an infallible certainty, but there is no doubt that Heidegger's thought about *Sein* is pervaded with disorder, bound to circumstantial historical episodes on which, through guileful contrivance, he wished to confer a philosophical excellence that they surely lack. Moreover, such a thought about *Sein* was presented in a language that, as has been noted, besides neglecting all semantic precision, subverts the traditional meaning of words by giving them another one that interferes and clouds arbitrarily the message that ought to come through diaphanously.

In Heidegger's hands, the art of playing with words became a *divertimento* with philosophical pretensions, which would vouch for the diffusion of his thought about *Sein* captured in a mystery whose secrets not only are beyond the reach of metaphysical intellection, but also endowed with an aura detectable only by those on whom had been bestowed access to its revelation in history. Among these, the German philosopher modestly reports, Heidegger himself is the happy repository of the truth of *Sein*, since the task to which he dedicated himself from the publication of *Sein und Zeit* was to think and rethink about it with the aim of determining what its essence consists of in spite of having been forgotten by the science of being as such. But the Heideggerian thinking about *Sein* is disappointing. It did not crystallize in any efficacious replacement for the irreplaceable metaphysics of natural reason. For this very reason, given that Heidegger did not resort to metaphysical reasoning to speculate about the

---

4   Cf. *Was heißt Denken?* p. 54.

act of being that makes everything be, he did not tell us what
the very essence of *Sein* is either. Max Müller, one of his most
enthusiastic admirers, shared the same opinion in saying that
Heidegger did not formulate any theory to answer the question about *Sein*.[5] The same conviction has been expressed
from many Neothomistic analysts of Heideggerian thought.[6]

Since Heidegger disliked metaphysics, his thought about
Sein shows itself as an esoteric gnosis intended to substitute
for the speculation of first philosophy a mystical idyl of consciousness in the ineffability of something unattainable which
he equivocally called *Sein*. Equivocally, because it is neither
the act of that which is nor the substance of the uncaused
cause that created everything that is not its own act of being.
Indeed, it is a gnosis because it discards every human possibility of understanding the act of being through the philosophical investigation of the things that are. This thought
proposes instead that *Sein* would reveal itself in history, yet
not by an act of a being whose essence is the very subsistent
act of being that made its intimate life known to the whole of
humankind, but through a mysterious communication that
would come into man's consciousness as a datum prior to
every understanding of the things that are. In turn, the esotericism of this gnostic thought about *Sein* is connatural to its
hermetic character, for the truth of *Sein* would have remained
concealed in the history of humanity until Heidegger, by
announcing it with an inscrutable symbolism, deigned to
transmit it to the coterie of recipients of his extra-metaphysical thought about *Sein*.

It is suitable to compare the thought-provoking nearness
of the revelation of *Sein* that Heidegger promoted to some
outstanding features of the so-called *apocalyptic literature* composed between the second century BC and the second century

---

5   Cf. M. Müller, *Existenzphilosophie im geistigen Leben der Gegenwart*, 2nd
     ed. (Heidelberg: F. H. Kerle Verlag, 1957), p. 115.

6   Cf. V. Possenti, *Approssimazioni all'essere* (Padova: Il Poligrafo, 1995),
     p. 84.

AD. This apocalyptic literature appeared as pieces that contained 'revelations' and also suggested that the past and the present would discover the future as something planned in the olden days.

> Apocalyptical authors devised a "literary vision" matured through study, but unrelated to the environments in which they lived . . . . They assumed an ecstatic attitude from which arose an experience closed in on itself, that explains why in that literature the monologue was prioritized. . . . Thus, esoteric transmission is invoked to explain why writings so venerable remained unknown for so many centuries and to legitimate the novelty both of the thought and the form of the alleged revelation they involve. . . . Apocalyptic authors had no interest in composing literary works of any originality, but they gathered together scattered materials taken from several traditions whose sources are now unidentifiable. . . . Hence, readers of the apocalyptical texts had the feeling of being faced with something as unattainable as it was ineffable. Intending to introduce this feeling in the reader's soul, the seer shows himself as someone inferior to the dazzling and admirable revealed realities. Of course, this enchantment required a vast catalogue of symbols which were used commonly as suitable devices to avoid the explicit descriptions of what was supposedly revealed . . . . Although these symbols have not been contrived by the seer's pusillanimity, he handled them cunningly to profit from their conventional usefulness. At all events, they were not invented as a result of any poetic inspiration . . . . Moreover, the symbology of apocalyptic revelations always included the exaggerated use of highly-colored metaphors and hyperboles destined to express the inexpressible and to accentuate the atmosphere of unreality in which these fictitious revelations are contained.[7]

---

7   A. Romeo, "Apocalittica (letteratura)," in *Enciclopedia cattolica*

No doubt, the philosophical knowledge of the act of being, as it is reachable through metaphysical speculation, does not meet these irrational and enigmatic standards, for they do not lead to the sapiential understanding for which philosophizing reason searches tirelessly. Nevertheless, legions of modern thinkers, of whom Heidegger is the most recent, have sought to insert them into philosophical life where they have no place; is this an effort to effect a turn of the human spirit from λόγος το μῦθος?

Metaphysics is the wisdom *par excellence* of natural reason, but it does not seek to exceed the humbleness of all human knowledge. It starts rudimentarily with the understanding of the things that we perceive daily through sense experience with the aim to know what and why they are. So we deduce that they are by the act that makes them be. But first philosophy notices something that raises it to the pinnacle of its sapiential theorization, i.e., provided that being is that which is, the concept of being is predicated of all the things that are. All things are represented by this concept, so that, in studying them insofar as things that are, the consideration of the subject of its speculations – being as such – makes clear that, even though all of them are, not every one of them is in the same way. Some things are in act and some in potency; some are in themselves and by themselves and others are in another thing; some are καθ' αὐτό, or *per se*, and others κατά συμβεβηκός, or *per accidens*, for being is predicated neither univocally, for it includes differences, nor equivocally, for notwithstanding the diversity of beings it excludes nothing that is. Therefore, being is predicated analogically, since the differences among beings do not abolish the likeness in which all communicate in the act of being which entifies them. Nevertheless, although all beings are, no worldly being is by itself, or by its own essence; moreover, every being of this kind is an effect consistent with its own act of being since this

(Città del Vaticano: Ente per l'Enciclopedia Cattolica e per il Libro Cattolico, 1948), vol. I, col. 1620–23.

act is not an attribute of its nature, but an act received thanks to the causative action of an extrinsic principle, itself uncaused, that gives the act of being to its effects without them demanding such a gift. And this stands to reason, because the act of being could not be given or communicated if the cause that gives or communicates it universally were a caused cause. Necessarily the universal and uncaused cause of the act of being of every effect is itself the very act of being. The act of being is the essence of this uncaused cause; otherwise, it could not give or communicate such an act, for only that which *is* the very act of being can cause all other things to be. So, whereas the things that have the act of being as something exercised finitely, once received as an act composed with their essences or natures, are beings by participation, the universal cause of the act of being is the being by essence that subsists eternally as a pure act because the act of being itself, the act of all acts and the perfection of all perfections, is its own nature. This is the being by essence, the subsisting act of being itself, whom all call *God*, metaphysically conceived as a being by analogy with the being that is not its own act of being, or that is by participation. This analogical conception of being implies the necessary resort to the principle of causality, for we gain knowledge of the being by essence from the knowledge of its effects. It also implies that we remove from its nature every imperfection of beings of this world, and moreover that we attribute to it supereminently, or in the utmost degree, all the perfections that caused things have in only a limited way. Yet this does not mean that metaphysics is a science of the divinity as such, for it is a theology that speculates about the being by essence in considering it only *sub ratione entis* or, even better, that does not deal with nothing but only with being as such. However, since metaphysics is a science, and since science is the true knowledge by causes, according to Aristotle's definition of epistemic knowledge,[8] first philosophy deals with the very

---

8   Cf. *Analyt. post.* Bk. I, ch. 2: 71 b 9–12.

subsisting act of being insofar as it is the most universal cause of every being that is not by its own essence.

This is metaphysics, the only science of natural reason fit to deal with that which is insofar as it is and also with the act of being by which are all the things that, in exercising such an act, are conceived as beings. We cannot think scientifically and philosophically about such an act beyond its condition of the act of being, and consequently beyond the epistemic field of the science of being as such. That is why, by having postulated an extra-metaphysical thought about *Sein*, Heidegger fostered a new gnosis marked by the estrangement of the very act of being in relation to the things that it entifies, while at the same time he denied that it is the uncaused cause of all the things of our universe. His trans-entitative *Sein* is not God. The universe would depend on an inexorably finite foundation that puts it at the edge of the abyss of a nothingness which would invite human reason, once bereft of a metaphysics crowned by the speculation of the very subsisting act of being, to despair as a failed potency of a soul naturally ordered to reach wisdom through its intellective union with the truth of the pure act. So the Heideggerian criticism of ontotheology, of an impossible metaphysics, represents the culmination of the occasionalist nominalism installed by Luther at the core of the agnostic catastrophe in which the Protestant spirit struggles.

Heidegger did not reject any particular current or school of metaphysics that had appeared in the history of Western philosophy; he rejected metaphysics *ut sic* by opposing to it the necessity of thinking about *Sein* independently of our scientific understanding of the things that are. The metaphysical speculation on the things that participate in the act of being and on the very subsisting act of being would be futile for that purpose. But it is time to ask if this marvelous creature that is human reason did suffer so morbid a historical blindness as to prevent it from reaching any knowledge of the truth of the act of being, to which the intellect is naturally ordered, until

Heidegger, in possession of a providential revelation, afforded the cathartic remedy for its inability to think about the mystery of the essence of a *Sein* concealed in things incapable of testifying to it. It is also proper to ask if the Heideggerian condemnation of metaphysics, because of its ontotheological vices, does not reproduce exactly Luther's incrimination of our discursive power, "the devil's prostitute," whose perverse historical influence never ceases to brand as haughty the desire to know God, the *ipsum esse subsistens*, through philosophical reasoning.

Due to its anti-metaphysical character, the Heideggerian thought about *Sein* is a pseudo-philosophical simulation of the religious drama of a thinker overwhelmed by the atmosphere of a civilization in which spiritual decadence goes hand in hand with the Protestant distortion of Christianity. The Christian confirmation of the truths reached by metaphysics through the natural use of human reason seems to mean nothing to those who gave up all hope of reaching rationally, albeit finitely and dimly, the truth of the act of being in harmony with the true divine revelation of the intimate life of the being by essence. The religious drama of a thinker who groped in the midst of the scraps of a thought of Christian roots, although despoiled illicitly of metaphysics, was manifest when he refused to nourish his thought with the metaphysical principles of natural reason and with the only sources of a faith always destined to understanding – *fides quaerens intellectum*. Once Heidegger gave up acceptance of the sources of the faith and metaphysical principles, he was driven to carry his thought back into the Pre-Socratic babblings of a philosophy soon to be plunged into the oppressive crisis of a reason ruled and tyrannized by logic. But logic would have failed in the same desert in which Western metaphysics dissolved at the hands of its last representative, that is, Nietzsche. Thus, the thought about *Sein* must find other sources. Plato and Aristotle were the fathers of the ontotheology that would make us enemies of the gods, that is to say, the same gods formerly revered in the thinking about *Sein* that Anaximander, Parmenides, and Heraclitus inaugurated. Pervaded with the glow of ontotheology, the results of Platonic and Aristotelian metaphysics must dissuade us from waiting for a God whom the philosophers would smuggle into the Christian tradition. These philosophers, besides having forgotten to think about *Sein*, would have thought a *causa sui* deity which deserves neither our prayers nor the offering of our sacrifices.[9]

The extra-metaphysical or extra-theological thinking about *Sein* is based on other and different sources. In the same way as Heidegger contested the metaphysics that Plato and Aristotle supported, he also sought to introduce mystery into *Sein*, by his devout visits to Hölderlin's Parnassus, a poet to whom Heidegger attributed an authority he in no way attributed to any philosopher. He perceived in Hölderlin's poetry the spirit of a new St. John the Baptist, as it were a hermeneutic key that would make it possible to ingratiate the *Sein* revealed in history, although never thought by metaphysicians. The German philosopher extolled Hölderlin's pantheistic muse with such unction that no one could distinguish it from a pagan mysticism full of bliss, a vivid sign of his predominantly affective, rather than philosophical or scientific, approach to the truth of *Sein*.

Doubtless these considerations could be rejected by appeal to several of Heidegger's texts that deny them outright. Why not? His works contain a permanent succession of unconnected and divergent opinions, sometimes fervently sustained, but later inexplicably abandoned, and, on the other hand, contradicted over and over again. In the same way that *Sein und Zeit* left behind the concerns of the young philosopher who haunted the Neoscholastic circles that abounded in his country during the first decades of the twentieth century, so we also see how in his thought the *Dasein*, the *Sorge*, and

9   Cf. "Die onto-theo-logische Verfassung der Metaphysik," in *Identität und Differenz*, p. 70.

the *Verfallen* have been overshadowed later in view of dealing with other kinds of problems. Nevertheless, from *Sein und Zeit* onward Heidegger intended to replace metaphysics with a thinking about *Sein* freed from the ontotheological constitution of the science of being as such. This thinking became the *Leitmotiv* of his literature. But what is this thinking about *Sein* that denies radically the possibility of a metaphysical speculation on the act of being? It is not a scientific knowledge, for this corresponds quintessentially to metaphysics, the *domina scientiarum* of philosophical tradition. It is not the knowledge of natural and positive social sciences either. Even less is it the knowledge whose principles are taken from divine revelation and recognized by faith. Ultimately, it is an experiment with thinking that pretends to work as a re-foundation of the entirely human thought on the alleged immanence of the truth of *Sein* in the very thought experienced by a subject who does not find in things themselves any evidence of such a *Sein*, which is to engage in a dialogue with thought in the hermetic intimacy of his own consciousness. But this attempt at an integral re-foundation of thought could not avoid eliminating first philosophy from the human soul, because the Heideggerian thinking about *Sein* was not only contrived under the influence of the immanentist and esoteric sources that captivated the German philosopher, but also based on a scathing criticism of philosophy as such, the science of truth and the supreme knowledge obtainable by man's natural reason, of which no one can say that it lacked magnificent and eminent expressions throughout mankind's pre-Heideggerian history.

Therefore, there are more than justified reasons to see in Heidegger's thought about *Sein* a gnostic mysticism whose aim is both to destroy the metaphysics of natural reason, something he propounded in *Sein und Zeit*, and of setting up a new thought from the subjectivity of the consciousness in which the question about *Sein* would inhere. In any case, consciousness would be in possession of a comprehension of *Sein* prior to the knowledge of anything that is.[10] This gnostic cadence of Heidegger's thought has been acutely noted by some philosophers who noticed not only its incompatibility with the only metaphysics of which the philosophizing intellect has any evidence, the science of being as such, but also its confrontation *vis-à-vis* with the true Christian mystics, for Heideggerian thinking about *Sein* shows itself involved in a neopaganism patiently presaged by the crisis felt throughout the more and more secularizing development of the spirit of Protestantism and of the very history of Reformation.[11]

Metaphysics survives placidly in spite of the thought that denies its epistemic and sapiential virtue to speculate about the act of being which makes everything be. Such a thought can dress up as philosophy, but at bottom it is the cry of a desperate consciousness which does not quite realize the limits of its finite capacity for knowing the infinity of the truth of the act of being within the smallness of human thought.

Metaphysicians have always dealt with the things that are thanks to the act of being that makes them be. On the contrary, Heidegger engages in a thinking about a *Sein* that makes nothing to be because it is not the act of the things that are, but a lonely inhabitant of a consciousness that would think about it, since the entire function of *Sein* supposedly consists of being thought by such a consciousness.

If the philosophical search for the truth of the act of being is excluded from the sapiential framework of metaphysics, or from the science of the first principles and the first causes of

---

10 Cf. *Sein und Zeit*, pp. 22–23. See the whole paragraph 6: "Die Aufgabe einer Destruktion der Geschichte der Ontologie," *Ibid.*, pp. 19–27.

11 See the clarifying remarks of L. Gardet, "À propos de Heidegger: valeur d'expérience de la 'question du sens de l'être'": *Revue Thomiste* 68 (1968) 381–418; and Y. Floucat, "L'onto-théo-logie selon Heidegger et l'immanence moderne au regard de la métaphysique thomiste," *Sapientia* 51 (1996) 187–229. Helmut Kuhn's judgments stated above (pp. 36–37) although formerly disregarded, were premonitory of the new evaluation to which Heideggerian thought is now being subjected.

things that are because of that act which entifies them; if, besides, it is undertaken without abiding by the canons of the logic that rectifies the scientific discourse of human reason, then it only remains for such a thought to devote itself to inventing a gnosis. Unavoidably, this gnosis must be imagined by a consciousness bewildered by hallucinations arising from an intellect divorced from its first uncaused cause and from the things to which it is naturally ordered to unite intentionally. Only in this way can man fulfill the deepest vocation of his soul, that is, to know the act of being which makes everything that participates in it to be.

Chapter VII

The Rejection of Metaphysics as a Regression to Gnosticism

Heidegger chose a thought about Sein that differs entirely from the speculation of philosophers who deal with this act. The difference that separates them indicates that they cannot be seen as two instances of philosophical knowledge except in an equivocal sense, since the German philosopher structured his thought about *Sein* to bring about a radical metamorphosis of the concept of philosophy and eliminate metaphysics once and for all. According to Heidegger, given that the science of being in common would be unable to think about the essence of *Sein*, or about *Sein* in its own purity, the task of thinking must belong to a thought that would think about *Sein* without any help from the failed attempts of Western ontotheology as founded in ancient times by Plato and Aristotle.

In comparison with metaphysical speculation, the most significant difference of Heideggerian thought about *Sein* is its exclusive dependence on thought's reflection on itself. Heidegger believed that in such reflection all the indispensable ingredients for carrying out the task of thinking about *Sein* would become manifest, at least insofar as this thought was protected from the vices involved in the structure of ontotheology.

Thought would perceive immediately its own thinking entity without needing any prior apprehension of anything different from itself, without needing to know anything existing in the external world before exercising its self-reflecting act. Thought would be informed intrinsically about its own entity, which would coincide exactly with self-consciousness.

In Heidegger's view, the thought and self-consciousness of the thinking subject are sufficient in themselves to discover in their intimate activity a λόγος that would involve itself with the matter of which thinking itself consists. This matter discovered in the intimacy of consciousness is nothing other than thought itself. The adoption of the monism once professed by Parmenides led Heidegger to praise its opportune recovery in Hegel's univocist system. Hence his agreement with the main theory of the Parmenidean-Hegelian theoretical association: Once thought finds the matter or thing of which it consists, *Sein* will become evident through a certain epiphany which would come about by the λόγος of a thought conscious of its own thinking entity. The correlate of this epiphany, so to speak, would be the thought itself which would seek to think about *Sein* in order to bring about their reciprocal conjunction in an original unity.

The *Sein* discovered by thought in its exercise of reflexive self-consciousness would not be grasped through knowledge of beings that participate in its actualizing power in the world outside the human soul. Rather, thought will discover it immanent to the consciousness of the thinking subject, because metaphysics, the ontotheology of traditional Western philosophy, has disclosed the inefficacy of any thought about *Sein* which would depend on the work of a λόγος ordered fruitlessly to thinking about itself in the presence of an ὄν that would conceal it, since not even the divinity of a being conceived as θεός would be capable of making evident the truth of a *Sein* ontologically different from the things which makes them be and be what they are, that is, from beings that are neither their own act of being nor the thought that thinks about it.

Therefore, Heideggerian thought aims to think about *Sein* as something immanent in the consciousness of the thinking subject as thought of thought itself. Then, both thought and *Sein* would allegedly constitute an original unity whose dissociation would not seem possible. Any attempt to dissociate them would senselessly repeat the failure of a metaphysics that sought to perceive *Sein* in the extra-mental objectivity of the beings in which it hid and eluded thought as long as it continued suffering the historical oblivion of the ontotheological exile to which Western philosophy condemned it in following Plato's and Aristotle's footsteps.

Once the epiphany of *Sein* is manifested by perceiving the thing or the matter of thought, thought itself would think about *Sein* in submitting it to a no-less-radical questioning, for *Sein*, according to Heidegger, would be something essentially questionable. This questionableness would be reduced to the *Seinsfrage*, i.e., the inquiry, the problem, or the question on *Sein* itself that would monopolize entirely the efforts of the thought aimed to think about itself.[1] All Heidegger's disciples agree with this theory. One of them, Karl Rahner, has expressed it through a statement that confirms the reach of the essential questionableness attributed to *Sein* by those authors who work under the influence of this master's thought.[2] Because he accepted the Heideggerian prolongation of Parmenides and Hegel's univocist monism, Rahner assumes that *Sein* and knowledge would join together, or perhaps would become identical, in their aforementioned original

---

1   Cf. *Sein und Zeit*, Introduction: "Die Exposition der Frage nach dem Sinn von Sein," pp. 2–40; and *Zur Seinsfrage*, 4th ed. (Frankfurt am Main: Vittorio Klostermann, 1977), reprinted in *Wegmarken*, pp. 379–419.

2   "To be is questionableness" (K. Rahner, s.j., *Geist in Welt: Zur Metaphysik der endlichen Erkenntnis bei Thomas von Aquin*, 3rd ed. [München: Kösel Verlag, 1964], p. 81. My translation.)

unity.[3] In turn, the questionableness of *Sein* would reflect the need for a questioning that thought would introduce into *Sein* itself in order to fit it to the revealing role of its truth. But ultimately the truth of *Sein* could not be revealed while it remained concealed in being. Therefore, the question about *Sein* would be destined to reveal its truth; not insofar as it stays hidden in the darkness of the things that are and forgotten by the ontotheological theorization of metaphysics, but in the measure that thought asks for *Sein*, in questioning it, starting from the shining comprehension with which it would inhere in the thinking subject's consciousness.

But, what is the problem of *Sein*? From *Sein und Zeit* onwards Heidegger insisted on the apparent necessity to solve this problem because, in his opinion, thought would perceive such a problem in the very essence of *Sein*, but he never said what that problem would consist of, nor was he able to offer any solution to solve it. It is only natural, because nobody can point the slightest questionableness in the act of being itself. This act is the proper act of being, but it is not a problem. All problems lie just on a thinker affected by limitations or deficiencies that deserve to be overcome, but, in this case, the problems affecting the thinking subject's mind do not move to the known things. That is why the questionableness Heidegger attributed to *Sein*, far from being inherent in it, can only be proposed as a function of the supposed transcendental capacity of consciousness to put something of itself into that which is being thought. In this sense, the essential questionableness of *Sein* reiterates obstinately the same statement through which, in his *Critique of Pure Reason*, Kant promoted a transcendental constitution of the objects of our thinking powers. At bottom, the questionableness of *Sein* propounded by Heidegger would require that thought pervade *Sein* itself with a questionableness which must derive necessarily from the very questioning thought. So, even though *in*

3   "So both to be and to know are in an original unity" (*Ibid.*, p. 82. My translation.)

verbis Heidegger would have denied it, his thought slipped unavoidably into idealism.

Thence one understands why Heidegger's immanentism, besides being at the antipodes of metaphysics, claims the absolute necessity of eliminating the science of being as such. Metaphysics by no means considers the act of being as a problem, but as the entifying act of the things that are and are what they are, beings, in which there is no problem at all, just as there is none in the act that makes them be. In the name of metaphysics, which does not tolerate any human thought introducing into external things a jot of entity, the external things that constitute the object of man's intellect – even though it be only a questionableness imagined by a thinking subject – St. Thomas Aquinas expressly opposed the kind of immanentism that we now find in Heidegger. Aquinas states: *Nihil intellectus est in intelligibili: sed aliquid eius quod intellegitur, est in intellectu.*[4] The Angelic Doctor thereby manifests that the only way thought could introduce any questionableness into the act of being is for the latter to be no more than a being of reason inhering in the thinking subject's intellect as a mere intentional form. In this case, the act of being would not be the act of the things that are, but a pure affection of man's mind. Consequently, one can see that the questionableness of *Sein*, such as Heidegger described it, has a clear and close connection with the conceptualist gnoseology once taught by Ockham, Suárez, Descartes, and Kant.

Since there is no way to determine the explicit content of the intrinsic questionableness Heidegger attributed to *Sein*, for it is not a question or a problem, such questionableness can only dissolve into a transcendental impregnation of the essence of that *Sein* on the part of thought, because thought is the only place wherein a problem can lie. Then, the true problem of Heideggerian thought about *Sein*, the fictitious questionableness contrived by a thought which, founded and constituted by the thinking subject's self-consciousness, considers

4   *De verit.* q. 8 a. 14 ad 5um.

itself empowered to think efficaciously about the truth of such a *Sein* while neglecting the causality of the external things knowable through man's apprehensive powers. But Heidegger did not concern himself with the extrinsic causality of the things of the outside world in relation to knowledge. His rejection of metaphysical understanding forced him to despise it over and over because such things are beings and, as such, are condemned to conceal their *Sein* which no ontotheology could reveal. But human knowledge claims an absolute necessity for the existence of knowable things outside man's soul. So how could that thought solve the alleged problem of *Sein* and reach its truth after having divorced itself from the things of the outside world that cause human knowledge?

The Heideggerian thought about *Sein* eschews understanding extra-subjective beings because they supposedly hide it and prevent it from grasping its truth. It is a thought that would subsist in its own entity as a thought freed from the things that are and, at the same time, fit to think about *Sein* itself by comprehending it in the subjective intimacy of the one who would think and question it independently of objective beings that would fatally obstruct its manifestation to the thinking consciousness. Nevertheless, this relationship of thought to *Sein*, which includes the agnostic attitude of a previous rejection of the knowability of such an act as something inherent in the very things that it entifies, also involves the assertion of *Sein* as the act of a solipsist consciousness that does not find in the outside world the object it is destined to associate with, that is, the very *Sein* thinkable by thought itself.

It is accordingly fair to ask if Heideggerian thought about *Sein* itself belongs to the cognitive order. Human knowledge is an act that necessarily requires an intentional union of a knowing subject and of its apprehensive powers with objects that are really distinct. Heidegger instead described thought about *Sein* as conformity to a nexus between themselves that can hardly be conceived properly as a cognitive assimilation. This is proved by the fact that, in Heideggerian literature, the mutual contact of thought and *Sein* always entails the presence of affective factors. In the last analysis, these affective factors turn consciousness into something similar to a scene of subjective experiences wherein knowledge of truth does not count at all; what does count is the therapeutic overcoming of *Dasein*'s emotional dilemmas. *Dasein*, someone supposedly thrown into the world by some unknown fateful principle, confronts its worldly destiny harassed by existential options that fluctuate between hedonistic delights and the tribulation caused by those other sinister things that overwhelm the spirit to the point of inviting it to despair.

Man would think about *Sein* as something inherent in the subjective consciousness because the beings that conceal its pristine truth do not satisfy the eagerness of a thought whose only consolation is to think about a *Sein* thinkable just by thought itself. Disappointed with the metaphysical stage of Western philosophy, his thought resists what must follow the knowledge of the act of all acts and of the perfection of all perfections, that is, the philosophical knowledge brought to culmination in the sapiential understanding of the first principle and the first cause of everything whose essence is really distinct from the act of being in which it participates in a finite and limited way. That is why the Heideggerian thought about *Sein* is not ordered to knowledge of God as it is available to the epistemic reason through the analytic argumentation of metaphysics. Rather it is simply ordered to *thinking*, i.e., to fortifying itself with the amicable and sympathetic presence of *Sein* as something inherent in consciousness, in the very place wherein knowledge might mitigate its loneliness – the morbid effect of its divorce from things and from the uncaused cause by means of which they are and are what they are – before the ineluctable agony of everything of which the *in-der-Welt-sein* would herald its extinction thanks to a triumphal nothingness.

The Heideggerian thought about *Sein* is imbued and dominated by an affectivity that precedes and even neutralizes the fundamentally noetic or cognitive nature of human knowledge. A thought that has resisted knowing the act of being by grasping the beings that are needs to justify its ordering to the thing with which it would be concerned – *Sein* as thought by thought itself –, in any event impelled by a subjective need that moves it to look for rest in something experienced as a *partenaire* endowed with a concrete affinity with thought itself. Ultimately, such a thought would think about *Sein* to palliate the tastelessness that would be implied in thinking itself without finding in self-consciousness any correlate, however small, of its own cogitative inclination. The Heideggerian rejection of the perception of *Sein* in the objectivity of the beings wherein it allegedly hides creates the necessity of sheltering it as something inherent in a subject that would guarantee the revelation of its truth through the only valid expedient to that end, that is, the very thought that would think about *Sein* itself, not only as the act of that which is, but as a splendid host of consciousness, in which it would be cognate with the very thinking that introduces it into consciousness itself by revealing its truth.

Heidegger portrayed a non-philosophical and extra-metaphysical thought about *Sein* as something that could well be called *experience by affective connaturality.*[5] It is enough to recall the passages in his writings where he used a vast repertoire of allegories aimed at transposing illusorily the passion of anguish into an experience that would reveal nothingness, even though a nothingness that, in spite of being nothing, nevertheless possesses an *essence* capable of rendering null

---

5   A comparison of the affective nature of Heidegger's thought about *Sein* with some aspects of the affective knowledge by connaturality, such as the Thomistic school deals extensively with it, would not be superfluous. Cf. J. Maritain, *Distinguer pour unir, ou les degrés du savoir,* 4th ed. (Paris: Desclée De Brouwer, 1946), pp. 489–573; and J.-H. Nicolas, O.P., *Dieu connu comme inconnu,* pp. 381–86.

and void the thinking subject. But metaphors are useless to mask contradictions. Heidegger had no problem in punning with the words *anguish*, *being*, and *nothingness* in order to sketch a rigmarole, or an anti-philosophical puzzle, which laid waste the importance of any rational coherence in his discourse. On the one hand, he affirmed that nothingness is a non-being, or that which is nothing, but, on the other hand, he also asserted that nothingness would have the virtue of causing annihilation. However, in spite of being nothing, for nothingness is not a being, anguish would make it evident. Now, how would anguish make evident a nothingness that is nothing? According to Heidegger, anguish would not disclose nothingness in making it evident as if it were a being or object, for anguish is not an apprehension of nothingness itself, but by revealing it to such an extent that there would be no difficulty about nothingness, since the non-being would be manifest within being itself, or within that which is.[6] The human weakness of our fallible reason forces us both to understand and to have compassion on the mistakes into which philosophers often fall, but it does not justify excusing them for the abuse implied in imagining that philosophy belongs to the genre of puzzles.

We are not entitled to regard the linguistic puzzles of Heidegger's vocabulary as a mechanism mischievously meant to confuse his readers. These puzzles simply arise from a thought that needed to symbolize with suitable signs the very same devious plot in which its noetical structure struggles against the conceptual and semantic repertoire of metaphysics. As a consequence of that, not even a methodic and patient reading of the works containing the Heideggerian thought about *Sein* ends by determining what is this *Sein* about which he speaks constantly. One reason for this is that he never declared explicitly its true character, another is that long-suffering readers of his works normally become exhausted in trying to puzzle out Heidegger's enigmatic

6   Cf. *Was ist Metaphysik?* p. 33, reprinted in *Wegmarken*, pp. 112–13.

language. As is well known, his language is directly proportionate to a thought enamored with an inscrutable *Sein* about
which Heidegger wished to think while avoiding the science
of being as such.

As was previously the case with Hegel, Heidegger seems
not to have given much to the deleterious presence of contradictions in his thought about *Sein*. An immanentist dialectic
that intends to solve every problem in the light of the laws
issued by a self-sufficient thought to rule its own thinking
activity, can even justify contradictions. Uninterested in the
adequacy of intellect to things – truth – it is content with the
subjective inclination of a thought aimed at satisfying both its
appetite for self-complacency and for being expressed in a
language compatible with its noematic structure.

Certainly, the embroiled language employed by
Heidegger to expound his thought about *Sein* is the congru-
ent result of the development of his own cogitations. In his
works, both thought and language are stereotyped in an
extensive range of metaphors and allegories. But these
metaphors do not correspond to the scientific nature of
authentic philosophy and eventually allegories just represent
aesthetically the affective outburst of Heidegger's cogitation.
It all ends finally in something similar to a mysticism destined to extol the ineffableness of a *Sein* which cannot be penetrated by epistemic reason. It is not a mere coincidence that
Heidegger described the thought about *Sein* as an amalgama-
tion of several human experiences whose psychical elements
include an undeniable emotive basis. For instance, when in
Rilke's honor Heidegger tried to enter into the sense of a
poet's work, *Sein* was described as something dissolved
anthropomorphically into man's affectiveness. Now, it is well
known that attitudes of this kind characterize constantly most
existentialist propositions, for existentialism believes that *Sein*
is immersed in a permanent adventure and that this adventure is *Sein* itself, so that *Sein* itself would be nothing other
that a mere adventure that poses for man the risk of becoming

beings.[7] Therefore, it is not surprising that Heidegger's writings exhibit an indissoluble marriage between his thought about *Sein* and the language he chose to signify it. Although semantics used to express philosophical theories has an obvious importance in the signification of intellectual conceptions, rarely does interest in language itself reach such an excessive height in the history of philosophy. But it is otherwise with Heidegger and language. He invented an *ad hoc* language to signify the thought about *Sein* with the aim of indicating that the *Sein* thought by thought itself would need a determinate place to shelter it, protect it, and put it at the disposal of those who wish to penetrate into its arcana. According to Heidegger, language would be the "temple" or "house of *Sein*" in such a way that language is that through which one must pass if one wishes to reach being through thinking.[8]

Nobody should be amazed by the fact that the language used to signify the Heideggerian thought about *Sein* plays exactly the same hermetic role once played by the semantics of ancient gnosis. Just as the gnostic spirit considered language to be a tabernacle in which to hoard both the wisdom revealed by the divinity and the science gotten by the human soul, so Heidegger has granted it a being that exceeds its symbolizing mission and made it a sacrarium in which *Sein* might disclose itself and radiate its truth to whomever introduces himself into the most recondite secrets of men's speech. Hence, in Heideggerian literature language appears as the

---

7   Cf. "Wozu Dichter?" in *Holzwege*, p. 257.

8   Cf. *ibid.*, p. 286. As it often occurs in many other Heidegger texts, in this one the capricious translation of τέμνειν as *tempus* also shows an exorbitant arbitrariness habitual in his writings, which adapt *a piacere* the meaning of Greek words for exploiting them to the advantage of his own points of view. Against Heidegger's translation, see H. G. Liddell & R. Scott, *A Greek-English Lexikon*. A New Edition Revised and Augmented throughout by H. Stuart Jones with the Assistance of R. McKenzie et alii, 9th ed., 6th rpt. (Oxford: Clarendon Press, 1961), s. v. τέμνω, pp. 1774b–1775a.

eminent testimony of the revelation of the truth of *Sein* and even as a garland of the oracles that it infallibly makes clear.

It is symptomatic, indeed, that notwithstanding his praise of language Heidegger never realized that human speech, in addition both to its communicational usefulness and to the beauty it can acquire by means of the perfection which human art may give to it, can also act as a transmitter of falsehood, lying, injury, impudence, and other vile things. In spite of that, Heidegger preferred to extol unilaterally the allegedly creative power of language; so much so, that it would be the defining thing in the rational animal's essence, whom he called the being "who possesses a language."[9] But, how far does the supposed creative power of the words of our language reach? The question is relevant, for whoever answers it must respect the dividing line that exists between metaphysics and mysticist delirium; otherwise, he will relapse anachronistically into the outlandish imagery of esoteric gnosis. Now, did Heidegger answer this question?

According to Heidegger, language is the house of *Sein* insofar as the words of human speech receive it as a guest in a place where its truth would be revealed, but, before giving it lodging, language would cause the entity of the things that are. Words and language would not simply be a mere symbolic cover, as the package of merchandise subject to business is. Inversely, once Heidegger echoed the gnostic criterion about the production of the very act of being of the things that are he held a doctrine whose alarming scope not only is capable of scaring philosophers, but even more capable of astonishing anyone who thinks he is living in a Christian era. Indeed, Heidegger said that *For us, only in the word, in language, do things exist and come to be.*[10]

The gnosticism involved in this Heideggerian confession is parallel to the anti-metaphysical regression of someone who paganized in a patently pantheistic sense the inaugural

---

9   "Wozu Dichter?" in *Holzwege*, p. 287 (my translation).

10   *Einführung in die Metaphysik*, p. 11.

revelation declared in the Gospel of St. John: *In principio erat Verbum, et Verbum erat apud Deum, et Deus erat Verbum. Hoc erat in principio apud Deum. Omnia per ipsum facta sunt, et sine ipso factum est nihil, quod factum est* (John 1:1–3). Gnosis plagiarizes these sentences literally, so that it announces without the least difficulty as well: *Omnia per ipsum verbum facta sunt, et sine ipso factum est nihil, quod factum est,* as is confirmed by Heidegger's utterance transcribed in the previous paragraph.

Probably it may be argued that Heidegger did not say that things are caused *by the word* but only that they are and come to be *in the word.* But this argument does not alter the terms of the question, because for things to be and come to be *in the word* it would be necessary that the subject who emits the linguistic signs – man – gives them the act of being that entifies them in the manner of a *conditor.* The argument does not clarify the gnostic character of Heidegger's ontogonic fantasy either, for in this case the act of being would even depend on the entifying action attributed both to the human being and to the productive causality of his words, so that it would not depend on the creative efficiency of the very subsistent act of being, or of the universal cause of everything that does not exist by virtue of its own quiddity but exercises the act of being by participation.

The gnostic character of this doctrine can be also perceived through another Heideggerian assertion entirely and ecstatically subordinated to Hölderlin's spiritual and theoretical authority, which deserves to be called such as it truly is: a grotesque rambling of the imagination. We refer to this assertion of Heidegger: "Man behaves as if *he* were the author and the owner of language, even though really it is *language* that is and has always been the lord of man."[11] It is not worth taking the trouble to reply to this statement which may dazzle

---

11 "Bauen, Wohnen, Denken," in *Vorträge und Aufsätze,* 5th ed., p. 140 (my translation). Heidegger reiterated almost *ad litteram* this statement in his essay ". . . Dichterische wohnet der Mensch . . ." (*ibid.,* p. 184).

someone poetically unhinged, but which is no less derisory in the light of sanity.

It is not sanity, precisely, that stands out in Hölderlin's life and works. Led by Hölderlin's hands, Heidegger ended up by confusing philosophy with an erratic dithyramb in order to think about things and *Sein* in the midst of the darkness of a language in which the esoteric gnosticism always comes together with the unintelligibility of ravings. Just an example is enough to make Heidegger's ravings evident: all men know that a jar is a recipient fit to contain material bodies and is commonly used to hold liquids, but if we ask Heidegger what a jar is, he, inspired in Hölderlin's poetic nonsense, tells us this: "The essence of the jar is the pure draining colligation of a simple Quaternion in a dwelling."[12] If that were so, mankind would have not known what a jar is until Hölderlin revealed the mysterious essence of his famous *quaternitas*, which allegedly works as the cause from which the *Sein* of a jar comes. At this point of this thought, Heidegger seems to have disbelieved that the uncaused cause of every participated act of being is the Triune God of Christianity, whose essence is the *ipsum esse subsistens* of metaphysics, the only author of this world in which we dwell and philosophize and where, besides, men make jars without giving them entities as odd as those that allegedly would emanate from the demiurgic work of that Quaternion, a myth which Heidegger accepted once enthralled by Hölderlin's captivating theosophic poetry. Now then, a thought that holds language, *our lord*, according to Heidegger, does not signify the existing things with the slightest diaphaneity, and, moreover, if the words of language were the 'house' wherein things would be and would come to be, is a thought whose frivolousness leads

---

12 "Das Ding," in *Vorträge und Aufsätze*, 2nd ed., vol. II, p. 46 (my translation). The German original of this veritable gibberish reads as follows: "Das Wesen des Kruges ist die reine schenkende Versammlung des einfältigen Gevierts in eine Weile."

indefectibly to poetic hallucinations that end up by defrauding the truth which philosophers seek and love vigorously. This is the end of the route which every gnosis follows ineluctably.

Once upon a time Heidegger planned to devise a thought about *Sein* under the influence of Hölderlin and Rilke, who incited him to seek in men's speech the secret of the foundation of everything, provided that things were not taken into consideration through metaphysical scientific speculation, but insofar as they are thought in the intimacy of a consciousness where they are covered by the peculiar decoration supplied by poetic language. This happened because Heidegger, among other omissions, did not carefully observe how imperative it is to recall the wholesome warning of Aristotle, paraphrasing an old proverb mentioned by Solon, in the *Metaphysics*, saying that "bards tell many a lie."[13] There is nothing more reasonable, because whenever man is not able to overcome the mere nominal signification of words, his thought ends up stuck in a mystification of language that follows from giving up speculation on the things that truly are.

Metaphysicians theorize on the act of being by investigating the causes of the subject of the science of being as such. Heidegger's gnosis instead discarded the syllogistic analytics of first philosophy because he propounded a thought which considers vainly to be itself of a philosophical nature, to such an extent that it does not consist of the knowledge of the things that are, but of a thinking about thought itself, just as Heidegger himself stated in plain language: "Philosophy did not arise from the myth. It arises only from thinking about thinking itself."[14] But if *a nosse ad esse non valet consequentia*, and if thought would be destined to think about itself, how could a philosophical discourse about *Sein* deduce why

---

13 Cf. *Metaphys.* Bk. I, ch. 2: 983 a 3-4. Cf. E. L. A. Leutsch & F. C. Schneidewin, *Paroemiographi Graeci* (Lipsiae: Teubner, 1839-1851), vol. I, p. 371, and vol. II, pp. 138 et 615.

14 "Der Spruch des Anaximander," in *Holzwege*, p. 325 (my translation).

things are and what is the act of being that entifies them? Heidegger's response to this question confirms the gnostic character of his thought about *Sein*, for the truth of the latter, which would have been fruitlessly sought by Western metaphysicians in the objectivity of the things that participate it, would lie in the poetic thought inherent in the consciousness of the thinking subject: "The poetic essence of thought preserves the reign of the truth of being."[15] Hence the thought about *Sein* would arise from a thought that would think about thought itself, in which the hermetic circuit of language would cause that which is and the very truth of being. Contrarily, according to Heidegger, Western metaphysicians would have forgotten to think about *Sein* by devoting themselves to speculation about things outside consciousness – the very beings – in which the truth remains hidden and can neither be signified through the creative word nor sung by poets.

In Heidegger's cogitative schema both man's thinking and speech fit together with the aim of outlining a new thought about *Sein* that would replace the metaphysics of Western philosophical tradition. Having disdained the causality of outside things, Heidegger emphasized thought and speech in order to explain how *Sein* could become manifest to human consciousness. Its manifestation would happen by means of a *revelation*, which, in conformity with its own nature, would exclude every apprehension of *Sein* through the natural evidences furnished by the intelligibility of the things that are because of the act of being. This revelation would have been made in history or in worldly events, to which *Sein* would be limited by its own finiteness. However, the historical revelation of *Sein* would not consist of the transmission of a message from a source extrinsic to the subject that exercises the act of thinking. Although Heidegger never indicates either the source or the message of this revelation, nevertheless it is clear that it would transmit the essence of *Sein* to the only thing capable of receiving it, that is, to

15   *Ibid.*, p. 303 (my translation).

thought itself, which is devoted to thinking about itself and to expressing it in a poetic way. Thought, according to Heidegger, possesses a poetic nature that renders unnecessary resort to any other artificial ποίησις foreign to its essence in order to become a saying, a speech, a word.

Thus, we may take it as established that *Sein* is alleged to be thought by thought itself and said by language whenever, once revealed to consciousness, the intellect would not know it objectively as the act of the external things speculated by philosophical reason. *Sein* would be thought both by a poetic thinking just verbally expressed and by a poetic speech as well that would imply, at least, the construction of that which would be thought and said, because every ποίησις is a making. It implies as well agnosticism with respect to the nature, purely and simply speculable, of the act of being. But such a theory moves one to ask: is the historical revelation of *Sein* a transmission to thought of a message whose content was unknown before it was revealed?

If thought did not know the *Sein* which would have been revealed in history, the grasping of the revealed truth ought necessarily to abide by the conditions of a formally speculative knowledge so that thought would think theoretically about *Sein* starting from a revelation incompatible with a thinking that thought poetically about itself since it would not have been made by thought itself. On the other hand, if thought thinks about *Sein* in exercising a poetic activity, a ποίησις that structures *Sein* as something effected by thinking itself, the following alternative presents itself: either the revelation of *Sein* is entirely superfluous, for it makes no sense for something to be revealed to thought if it can be made by thought itself, or such a revelation would not be anything other than thinking about *Sein* poetically. In our opinion, the second alternative is the only way in which Heidegger's enigmatic revelation of *Sein* can be understood, i.e., *Sein* reveals itself to consciousness historically insofar as it is thought in a poetic way by a thought that precisely thinks and says what arises from its cogitative efficacy, which is founded on the original unity of thinking and being.

As it has been said, Heidegger's esoteric gnosis is an anachronistic regression to Parmenides' univocist monism. Heidegger sought to justify it by admitting the extreme immanentist systematization that Hegel proposed within the context of a discipline equivocally called *Logik*. However, without betraying the spirit of Hegel's dialectics, Heidegger preferred to present his thought on *Sein* with the support and authority he attributed to Hölderlin's poetry, who summarized skillfully the marrow of Protestant theosophy in accentuating its neopagan features, and then on top of all that in promoting the ruin both of the Christian faith and of metaphysical understanding by means of an invitation to men to revere deities contrived in the heat of pantheistic opprobrium.

Summing up, this is our conclusion: Heidegger's thought about *Sein* reflects the abandonment of human reason for a poetic mysticism powerless to reach sapiential knowledge of the act of all acts and of the perfection of all perfections.

Epilogue

The apocalypse of *Sein* described by Heidegger is not the revelation of Him who made his intimate life known to humankind in saying of himself: "I am who am" (Ex 3:14). Nor is it the manifestation of the act by which the things of the world around us are, as that act can be apprehended by philosophical reason in metaphysical speculation on being as such, for the act of being of these things is not manifested through any revelation, but through the natural evidence of that which it makes to be. Therefore, the Heideggerian apocalypse of *Sein* is the discovery of the intentional immanence of its sign by the consciousness of a subject who would think about himself by thinking about his own thought. Such an apocalypse comes about along with the manifestation of a *Sein* thought by thought itself, about which it would think poetically, that is, creating the ποίησις of its thinking activity. Thus, the apocalyptic manifestation of *Sein* would depend on a transcendental construction, i.e., in the very sense that Kant granted to the word *transcendental*.

Heidegger had two reasons to postulate the revelation or apocalypse of *Sein*: his rejection of metaphysics or ontotheology as the science which deals with it, and his exegesis of the theory of the original unity of *Sein* and thought which Parmenides proposed and Hegel exalted to the highest degree. Given that metaphysics, according to Heidegger, failed as a thought about *Sein*, we cannot think about it while it remains concealed in being. *Sein* would only be thinkable insofar as its extra-entitativeness is allowed to reveal itself to thought. On the other had, if it could not be reached within the being that hides it, and if everything outside thought is a being, then the human approach to *Sein* would be guaranteed insofar as it inheres in a thinking consciousness. Consequently, the announcement of the revelation of *Sein* follows simply from Heidegger's failure to speculate on it in conformity with the epistemic analytics of metaphysics.

Heidegger invented the apocalypse of *Sein* because the immanentism in which all his thinking lies prevented him from understanding that human reason is naturally ordered to the knowledge of the things that are. Nevertheless, since perfect knowledge comes to the intellect by obtaining the habit of science – the certain knowledge of things through their causes – human reason can know such things perfectly by only apprehending their causes. Now, among all the causes of things stands out the principle by which they are, the act of being, so that perfect knowledge of them implies understanding the act that makes them to be by constituting them as beings. But the rational animal does not know the act of being by means of any revelation or apocalypse, but through natural intellection insofar as such an act inheres in the very things that it itself entifies by giving them their *raison d'être*. Thus I know that the stone is without receiving any revelation of its act of being. The theoretic development of first philosophy lies in the natural process of human intellective knowledge, which Heidegger rejected. The agnostic prejudice in his doctrine of the concealment of *Sein* in being moved him to deny that *Sein* may be thought as the act of that which is and thus knowable through the analytics of the science of being as such. *Sein* would not be *known* through the philosophical argumentation ordered to understanding the deepest of the things that are, in which the demonstrative power of metaphysical knowledge consists, but, at most, it would be *thought* insofar as it is revealed to the cogitative consciousness as a function of thinking of a poetic character, that is, of a thinking – whether or not Heidegger's admirers agree – that would constitute itself transcendentally or, if one likes, poetically. The ποίησις of Heideggerian thought about *Sein* is a mere emulation of the transcendental of Kant's *Critique of Pure Reason*.

Why did Heidegger invent this absurd apocalypse of *Sein*? There is no way of finding out the recondite personal reasons that led him to try to replace metaphysics with an esoteric gnosis emerging as the thought about *Sein* we just outlined. It is clear that this gnosis derived from Heidegger's disappointment in the intelligibility of the only things that naturally attest the entifying act of everything which is not its own act of being, and from his reviling of Western philosophy as a whole, and also from the mystic enchantment Hölderlin's seductive pantheistic theosophy caused in his spirit. But these are modest and insufficient clarifications of why Heidegger chose to lucubrate about an apocalypse of *Sein* that he was the first in history to perceive. The hermetic plot of his thought about *Sein* will always be an insuperable obstacle for anyone wanting to find out what is the root of his unusual regression to a gloomy gnosis which the fraternal alliance between metaphysics and the Christian faith thwarted many centuries ago.

Heidegger was an extraordinary thinker. The mistakes and wanderings enclosed in his thought about *Sein*, almost always plunged into a disorder comparable to the *confusio Babylonica*, deserve a firm and justified criticism, but it does not eliminate the obligation to notice in his thinking the amazing power of human reason, even if used for nothing else but concocting incredible chimeras. Nevertheless, the recognition of the extraordinary thinker that Heidegger was does not imply that one must see in his thought about *Sein* a philosophical contribution properly. He was simultaneously an extraordinary thinker sporadically disguised as a true philosopher, for he did not grasp the fundamental differences that exist between genuine philosophizing and mere thinking, between a lover of the truth of things and a passionate adorer of the thought immanent to a thinking subject's consciousness.

Index